THE NEXT AMERICAN PRESIDENT

THE NEXT AMERICAN PRESIDENT

—————

Fred Seaman

This book is dedicated to Eric and Gail, the two best kids a guy could ever hope for. They are the best of the good parts of my life.

Acknowledgments

———

THANKS TO MY MENTOR AND cheerleader, Karyn Rae.

Brendon Steenbergen, thanks for the awesome cover art.

LT. Mike Bell, United States Coast Guard, a super professional and knowledgeable gentleman.

Michael P. Riley, tough, intelligent, and always an inspiration.

TABLE OF CONTENTS

"The liberty of a democracy is not safe if the people tolerate the role of private power to a point where it becomes stronger than their Democratic State itself.

"That, in its essence, is Fascism, ownership of Government power by an individual, by a group, or by any controlling power, other than the people themselves."

– President Franklin Delano Roosevelt

INTRODUCTION

"Democracy does not guarantee equality of conditions;
it only guarantees equality of opportunity."

— IRVING KRISTOL

AMERICA IS A NATION OF mixed breeds and mutts. I doubt that there are many thoroughbreds among us, and that is why this is the greatest nation on Earth. We have walked on the moon, cured many diseases, and helped almost every other nation on Earth in one way or another. We have been the world's poster child for freedom, liberty, democracy, and justice for all of our people.

"The land of the free" and "the home of the brave" are not just words in a song. It's how we live.

You can see the beauty of this country in our mountains, our rivers, and our fields, which stretch to the horizon. You can feel our heartbeat in the rhythms of our dynamic cities. You can see the essence of our indomitable spirit in the faces of our citizens.

The sad part of our story is that we have lost a great deal of the good of our country, and we will lose all of it in the next few years. We were not overcome by terrorists or outside influences of any kind. We have let a few ruthless, unpatriotic, greedy, and selfish people in our own country buy the souls of our elected officials. Today, anything that happens in Washington, DC, is for the good of the wealthiest 1 percent of our population. For the rest of us, our way of life is in real jeopardy.

A recent poll showed that 86 percent of our citizens agree that our so-called leaders are completely out of touch with mainstream America, and they are bought and paid for by special-interest groups. Only 9 percent thought that our problems could actually be solved. That 86 percent also believes America has seen its best days, and it will be downhill from here. They said they were very fearful of the conditions that their children and grandchildren will have to endure in the coming years.

How can this exist in a democracy?

Actually, this condition only exists because we the people *let* it exist. We have the power to solve these problems very quickly and easily, but we have been so skillfully lied to by the selfish, greedy folks who are only interested in their own net worth that we don't realize what Washington is doing to us. And we don't realize how simple and attainable the remedies are.

So, what steps do we have to take to regain control of our country and get it moving in the right direction?

The first thing we have to do is make sure that all our people understand the true nature of the situation in which we find ourselves. Special-interest groups representing the greedy among us have been waging a disinformation campaign for many years, designed to divert our attention from their efforts to take control of our country. They have been very successful in getting us to believe that our problems stem from the federal government itself. They have convinced us that the actual conflict is between our government and our citizens.

It's true that our government is not perfect. But neither is it designed to be our enemy. Our government is merely the working arm of a democratic society that is supposed to do the bidding of our citizens. The special-interest groups have put together a highly sophisticated campaign to convince us that the federal government is our biggest enemy, when in reality, those groups are quickly taking control of it.

If we are to survive as a democratic nation, of the people, by the people, and for the people, we must do the following things before it's too late.

First, we must convene a constitutional convention that ***sets term limits for members of Congress and the president of only one five-year term.***

This constitutional convention must also establish a ***balanced budget amendment*** that precludes lawmakers from taking us into debt.

Recall petition procedures must be included in the constitutional amendment, giving the voters the power to remove any federal office holder from office in a timely and permanent manner.

We also need to ***prohibit any present or past federal elected officials from accepting any payoffs, bribes, or gifts of any kind.***

The amendment also needs to set a ***limit of $100*** for any contribution to any political campaign by any person, firm, or corporation. All campaign contributions must be reported to a campaign ethics commission within forty-eight hours.

Most of all, we need to elect regular, everyday Americans as our leaders. We must get away from the professional politicians who are marketed like tubes of toothpaste and are completely beholden to their greedy contributors. It is those contributors who want to own our country.

These are the simple, common-sense changes that need to be made in order to deliver the power and control of our country back to its citizens. While this may seem an arduous task, it pales in comparison to the hardships our forefathers had to endure in the formative years of our country. None of these changes requires that we starve and freeze at Valley Forge or fight and die during the years of the Revolutionary War. We will not be required to do anything dangerous. We do not need to lay down our lives, as hundreds of thousands of our forefathers had to.

All we have to do to save our country is sign petitions, contact our elected officials, and vote. It's a small price to pay to live in the greatest country on the face of the earth.

CHAPTER ONE

THE INAUGURATION

———◆———

*Some people run for public office because
they want to **be** something. Others run
because they want to **do** something.*

IT IS A COLD DAY in Washington, DC. Dark clouds and a swirling mist are starting to cover America's capital. A strong north wind gives promise of rain as the inaugural procession starts down Pennsylvania Avenue. As the clouds become darker and more menacing, they seem to warn of the days to come for our country.

A polished full-bird colonel in a complete dress blue uniform says, "It's time to go, Mr. President" for the third time, and I still can't believe he's talking to me. Three Secret Service agents start to move, herding me like a lost sheep into the presidential limousine. In a way, Barack Obama seemed relieved to pass the torch to me, and we chatted on the way from the White House to the Capitol building. He was actually a very friendly guy, and he gave me several tips on things to do as president and things to avoid at all costs. Congress seemed to be the main one to avoid.

This trip had actually begun twenty-four months ago, caused by a strange twist of fate that had changed me from a small-town, everyday guy into a household name overnight—further proof that no good deed goes unpunished.

As the motorcade picks up speed, I search my pockets for the inaugural address for the twelfth time. On a single piece of paper, I've scribbled out my thoughts for the day on which I am to become the forty-fifth president of the United States. Short, straight to the point, and honest. The American people and, for that matter, the rest of the world had better get used to short and not necessarily sweet. That's the only way I know how to do things.

In 2017 America, words from our political leaders have become catchphrases, sound bites, and politically correct milquetoast, designed to be exactly in the middle of the road, to offend no one, and to stay as far away from truth or controversy as possible.

Like most other average Americans, I have felt strongly for many years that our beloved country needs a change of course, a change in leadership philosophy, a new direction to head in. Without these, our way of life will deteriorate into extinction in the next very few years. It's time for real change.

Well, listen up, Mr. and Mrs. America. There's a new sheriff in town.

I ask the well-dressed, intelligent-looking Secret Service agent sitting across from me in the limo if it is always this cold in Washington on Inauguration Day.

He replies, "The warmest inauguration on record was Reagan's first, at fifty-five degrees, and the coldest was his second, at seven degrees."

Damn, these guys are good! I wonder if he can shoot that well, too.

The swearing in ceremonies were to take place on the Capitol's west front, on a ten-thousand-square-foot platform engineered to hold 1,600 happy people.

As we walk up to the inaugural platform and start shaking hands with the assembled dignitaries, I notice the huge crowd assembled on the street below. The fact that they are here on such a nasty day is a testament to the fact that America has been ready for a change—real change this time—and its citizens are here to see that change become reality.

As I place my hand on the family Bible, opened to Psalms, to take the oath of office, the full weight of what has transpired in the last year finally settles into my mind. This is really happening. In just a little over a year, I have transformed from an everyday, middle-class guy into the most powerful man in the world. My emotions run from exhilaration to fear, to confidence and resolve, like the ball in an old-fashioned pinball machine.

While repeating the words of the oath of office after the chief justice of the Supreme Court, I feel a resolve settling into every part of my being. Yes, by God, we will change things—for the better, for the middle-class Americans who made this country great in the first place.

Presidential inaugural addresses historically have run the gamut from very short to unbelievably long, and from elegant to really bad.

My single-piece-of-paper speech squarely addresses that fact. I begin:

"Historians tell us that the shortest inaugural address in American history took place on March 4, 1793. It was given by George Washington at his second inauguration and was only 135 words long.

"He went on to become known as the father of our country.

"The longest speech was delivered by William Henry Harrison, on March 4, 1841. It was 8,495 words long, and it lasted for one hour and forty-five minutes. He died thirty-two days later, from pneumonia contracted during that long exposure to weather similar to what we have here today.

"I can assure you that my words today will be much more like the former than the later."

The small titter of laughter that runs through the assembled crowd is not nearly as much as I had hoped for, but supposedly there has never been even one word of humor intentionally written into an inaugural address.

There you go. I am already upholding tradition.

I go on to honestly and profusely thank all of those who worked on the campaign, contributed money, voted for me, or helped in any way to bring about the totally unbelievable installation of a common, every day, middle-class person into the highest office in the land.

I then talk about the dramatic changes that have to come if we are to survive and thrive as a nation, and I explain that I can't accomplish all these things by myself. The American people, by electing me, have just begun the job of taking back our country from the hands of the powerful and greedy special-interest groups, which have been systematically raping our country and its citizens for such a long time. These groups have illegally and immorally tightened their grip on our government for the last fifty or so years, without the slightest care or concern for the millions of everyday folks who have done the heavy lifting to make this the great nation it is today.

I describe these people as heartless, greed-driven individuals with no care for anyone or anything except the constant increase to their already obscene fortunes and ever-increasing stranglehold on the elected leaders of our country. "They are much more dangerous than the foreign terrorists" are my exact words.

I sum up this part of my speech by quoting from Franklin Delano Roosevelt's second inaugural address: ***"The test of our progress is not whether we add more to the abundance of those who have much: it is whether we provide for***

those who have too little. I then jump forward in time and quote Rachel Maddow: ***"This is not the time to give up on Washington. Now is the time to prove the political processes works." Damn straight, Rachel!***

The most important part of the speech, not to mention of my presidency, is to make sure that everyone in the entire world knows what my goals are.

"It is my intention that the next four years will be a period during which all of the resources of the federal government will have only one goal, and that goal will be to provide the best possible service to *all* of the citizens of this great nation. We will do so with courtesy, respect, and proficiency. That will be the hallmark of the executive branch of your government, and it must also be followed by the legislative and judicial branches.

"The day of serving two masters is gone. Everyone in a leadership position must be completely focused on the good of all the people. America cannot long survive if those in its leadership positions are completely controlled by special-interest groups or by considerations of their own welfare. We must show respect for all the people of this great nation and work together in a spirit of cooperation if we are to achieve the goals that the people sent us here to accomplish.

"Many will say that we are naïve to actually believe that these things can be accomplished, in light of what has been going on in Washington for the past several decades. But I say this: if we, the elected representatives of the people, can't accomplish the people's bidding, then we don't deserve to be here.

"I pledge to every American citizen right here and now that I will try my absolute best to provide the very best government of the people, by the people, and for the people. Should I not be able to accomplish this goal, I will not see this experiment in democracy fail. I will go straight to the boss.

"A lot of folks in this city seem to have forgotten who the boss is. But I haven't forgotten, and I never will forget that in a democracy, the power lies with all of the people, all of the time. If this administration encounters obstacles that prevent it from accomplishing the things necessary to create and preserve the best possible quality of life for all Americans, then I will take these issues to the only people who have the final jurisdiction to deal with them: the American citizens, taxpayers, and voters."

That will probably get the attention of some of the dinosaurs shuffling around the capital, who think they rule by divine right.

———

Amazingly, the ceremonies went off quickly and without a hitch. It was actually fun riding in the limo, walking the streets, and waving to the crowds. My son and daughter and their spouses seemed to be enjoying this part of the proceedings. They had looks of wonderment on their faces as we walked together hand-in-hand down Pennsylvania Avenue, between lines of ecstatic and noisy well-wishers ten and twelve deep.

The traditional congressional luncheon, held in Statuary Hall in the Capitol building with the leaders of the House and Senate, had been very similar to taking an ice-water shower. They knew full well the platform I had campaigned on and what its impact on them was going to be in the upcoming years. The lines were already drawn, and there was no pretense of friendship, no effort toward civility. Just cold, short sentences. And the food was pretty damn crummy, too.

After the traditional reviewing of the parade from the North Lawn of the White House, we were finally able to go inside what was to be my home for the next four years. The former president and his family had left right after the inaugural speech and were on their way into our nation's history. In just a few hours during the inauguration and parade, a team of enthusiastic people had removed all signs of the former occupants. During the official transition, I was asked what changes I wished to have made in the White House décor and furnishings, and I replied, "Just change the sheets. I'm here to fix Washington, not redecorate it."

Tonight was shaping up to be probably the biggest party night of my life. There were to be three official inaugural parties, complete with food, beverages, bands, and dancing. I had gotten to choose the entertainment. I'd picked the Eagles for the first party and asked that they play "Hotel California" and "Witchy Woman." For the second party, I had picked ZZ Top and requested "Cheap Sunglasses," "Sharp Dressed Man," and "Gimme All Your Lovin'." Saving the best for last, I had asked for Fleetwood Mac to play the last party and start off with "Edge of Seventeen," then play every song from the *Time Space* album, which I had listened to about a million times in the last thirty years.

Yep, I am a seventies rock and roller, and proud of it.

Dancing with my daughter was tricky—she had taken or taught several kinds of dance for twenty-five years, and she was better than good on her feet.

Lots of happy people were enjoying heavy hors d'oeuvres, great music, and dancing. And yes, Stevie Nicks was still hot. Dancing with her twice was worth all of the hardship of the campaign. She was completely weightless, the essence of gracefulness as we seemed to float across the dance floor. The scent of her perfume brought back forty years' worth of old memories from her music and videos, and it was terrific to feel like a carefree teenager again. It was truly a night to remember. If the next four years proved to be as much fun as this night, it was going to be a hell of a job.

There were several attractive ladies who looked like they might want to dance with the first single president to be inaugurated in 132 years. One in particular kept giving me that "come hither" stare and smile. As I realized that she was half my age and strikingly beautiful, the chump alarm in the back of my head started making its normal little "you better not do that" noise. This very possibly might have been an attempt by some of my political enemies to stick me in the trick bag on my very first day in office. I had mentioned during the campaign that wariness was one of the necessary qualifications of a potential president, and I decided to take my own advice.

So instead of following my natural instincts, I made it a point to dance with each of the wives of the Joint Chiefs of Staff. My first official act as president would be to meet with the Chiefs the next morning at ten o'clock, and I wanted to thank their wives for their service to our country. I knew they had sacrificed a great deal during their lives for the good of our country, just as their husbands had. I might as well get off on the right foot for the next day's meeting.

As my kids, their spouses, and I arrived at each party, I made my short thank you speech, wished everybody well, and advised them to have a great night but to be up and ready in the morning because we were all going to go to work for the good of the citizens, voters, and taxpayers of this great country. Everyone was in a high state of euphoria, and the striking brevity of my speeches was forgiven if not appreciated.

The whole night could be summed up in one word: awesome.

After the parties were over, I lay in a strange bed, in a strange house, with its strange noises. My mind was processing information at top speed. Sleep was not anywhere in the picture.

I kept thinking about a letter I had received from a history professor at a Midwestern university. He had congratulated me on my election and provided a historical ranking of all the presidents since George Washington. It seems that I was the fourth tallest president, the sixth heaviest, and the second old-est (by a year and a half) ever to be elected. Having served one term on the city council back in my small hometown, I had spent by far the least amount of time in elected office of any president, except Washington himself. According to the pro-fessor's research, I was one of only two presidents to be single on Inauguration Day. He thought that I was the ninth best public speaker and twenty-third best dresser, and I had the eighth best hair. That was where I started to doubt him. I thought Kennedy and I were probably tied for first place in the hair department. The first thing I would be doing in the morning was hair checks on the portraits of former presidents that hung all over the White House.

He also went on to give his opinion as to why the leadership of our country was so terribly dysfunctional, and I agreed with him completely. The problems we faced were represented by our fictional wars with Canada and Albania. If you do not remember these two wars, it is because you missed the movies about them.

In 1995, Michael Moore produced a comedy called *Canadian Bacon*, starring Alan Alda as a president of the United States with a terrible popularity rating. He starts a fake war with Canada to divert everyone's attention from his pitiful performance as presi-dent. In 1997, the movie *Wag the Dog* told the hilarious story of an incumbent president who gets caught making advances toward underage girls two weeks before the election. Dustin Hoffman and Robert De Niro cook up a fake war in which we are supposedly attacked by Albania, to divert the voters' attention from the truth.

While these two movies were only Hollywood comedies, they were perfect examples of what was going on with our political system.

The important issues that our leaders should have been focused on were: the economy, terrorism, immigration, quality health care, crime, the environment, a foreign policy that would give us the respect of other nations, and our infrastructure. And, basically, the things that affected the daily lives of average American citizens.

The nightly news informed us that our leaders were completely focused on abortion, LGBT rights, gun control, and being adamantly opposed to anything that the other political party dared to mention. Although these issues were important (except for the last one), the government couldn't legislate citizens' opinions and change conditions. These issues themselves become a permanent, reoccurring smokescreen for the purveyors of disinformation.

Thus, members of Congress could divert voters' attention away from the fact that they had no interest in solving the actual problems the average citizen faced every day. At the same time, they could pick up the unwavering financial support of a myriad of special-interest groups.

What was actually happening was that our elected leaders would have reaped no benefits from fixing the problems that affected us directly. In order to garner a following and fill their campaign war chests, they threw up the smokescreen of us against them, red versus blue, conservative versus liberal, Republican versus Democrat, and, worst of all, any religious group versus people who didn't believe in exactly the same things that they did.

These were not the things that divided America. The great divide in America was between the average citizen and our elected officials.

———

Having been semiretired for the last several years, I was not used to any type of wakeup call or alarm clock, and the buzzing of the telephone beside my strange bed, with its clean sheets, awakened me with a start. Not having the slightest idea of where I was, was unsettling, to say the least.

I looked around the strange room wondering where my old, scratched-up chest of drawers was, and I tried to find the source of the constant buzzing. I finally located the source of the annoyance: a strange-looking telephone next to the bed, with a blinking light begging for attention.

"Hello?"

"Good morning, Mr. President, this is your six o'clock wake-up call," said a cheery voice on the other end of the line.

Mr. President? Six o'clock? Are you shitting me? I hadn't been up at six o'clock in years. I looked around the gigantic bedroom and remembered where I was and why I was there.

"Thank you," I said into the phone, making a mental note to find out where the cheery voice was located. I hated talking to people on the phone that I'd never seen in person.

As soon as I hung up, there was a polite tapping on the door. I threw on my robe and told the dogs to stay, as a short gentleman with a giant smile and a pleasant demeanor came through the door with a tray of hot coffee.

"Good morning, Mr. President," he said in a deep tenor.

This was going to be much better than stumbling around in my house back in the Midwest, with bare feet on cold floors, making my own coffee. I wondered if any of the previous residents of this house appreciated these perks. Probably not. They were mostly well off folks and used to the finer things in life, which the rest of us had never experienced.

I showered, shaved, dressed, and quietly opened the bedroom door to see what my new life had to offer. And there it was, three Secret Service agents and a very large marine gunnery sergeant in full dress blues.

"Good morning, Mr. President," they all said in unison.

The marine stayed put, and the Secret Service and I took off down the hall, around the corner, down another hall, and around another corner. We stopped.

"Just exactly where in the hell is my office?" was my first official question since taking office.

"Please, follow me, Mr. President," said the tallest of the Secret Service agents without even a hint of a smile. We backtracked.

I checked out a couple of former presidents' portraits—yep, bad hair—and then we made a right turn and went through the door titled Oval Office.

"Good morning, Mr. President," I heard from four secretaries; my chief of staff, Mike; the press secretary; and three other people I didn't really remember, all at once. This was going to take some getting used to. Having lived by myself for the last twenty years, I normally didn't hear a human voice until after my third cup of coffee in the morning, and that was usually on the telephone.

Mike, tall and thin, with receding sandy hair, was the most intelligent and mentally toughest person I had ever met. He was not just my attorney; he was my friend and confidant from back home. He had never cut me any slack on anything, and I trusted him implicitly. He held degrees in both engineering and law and had a gigantic IQ, but his long suit was common sense. He could understand complex issues instantly and come up with sensible solutions as fast as people could present the information to him. His personality and bearing commanded immediate respect from everyone he came into contact with—and generated a great amount of fear in other attorneys.

He was a natural for any position in the administration, but I needed him most as my chief of staff, so he would be close at all times. After only two months of constant arguing and begging, he agreed to take the job with the proviso that upon our first serious disagreement, he would be on the next plane back home.

He immediately took charge, as I knew he would. He ushered me into my office and said, "You're early for your meeting with the Joint Chiefs of Staff."

"Good, let's have a beer."

Mike had never appreciated my sense of humor, and the dirty look he shot me made me happy that I could still irritate him so quickly. I watched as he stifled the urge to preach me a sermon on the importance of presidential propriety, and instead asked what I had in mind for the meeting with the Chiefs.

"Well Mike, It's my hope that I will be a peacetime president, working on the problems that affect every day Americans. But before I can do that, we are going to have to stomp out this terrorism shit ASAP and permanently. I intend to deliver that message to the Chiefs this morning and make them understand that is their job, and they need to get on it—with the full backing of the office of the president—right now."

Mike started talking, but the words blurred and faded as my senses took in the grandeur of the Oval Office. The sense of all the world-changing events that had transpired in this office in the past floated through my mind, like the spirits the Indians believe in. My next thought was *what in the hell am I doing standing in this office*, and my thoughts drifted back to the day this whole process started . . . .

———

On a warm, sunny summer day, I was driving on the two-lane highway going north out of our quiet little town, when an SUV in front of me slid off the road and overturned in a ditch. Smoke started rolling out of the upside-down vehicle as I slammed on my brakes and slid to a stop on the shoulder of the road, twenty yards behind the wreck.

As I ran toward the vehicle, I could hear a woman and her child screaming. Bright orange flames started to lick out from underneath the hood. I reached through the broken driver's side window and jerked on the door handle, opening the door with a jolt.

The woman was hanging upside down by her seat belt, and blood was running off her face and dripping down into the roof of the car. I pushed on the seat belt release mechanism as hard as I could, but her weight against the strap made it impossible to release the belt.

Luckily, former farm boys carry pocketknives. I took mine out and cut the seat belt with one hand, while breaking her fall and guiding her down and out of the vehicle as gently as possible. She lay there cradled in my arm, moaning, "My baby, my baby." So I turned my attention to the screaming child in the backseat. He seemed uninjured but frantic.

Cutting him out of his car seat was much more difficult than cutting her seat belt had been, especially since the car was filling with acrid smoke and I could feel the heat of the flames as they got closer to my bare arms. I wanted away from the searing heat and billowing smoke, but her eyes were large, deep pools of fear and desperation. They kept me at the task at hand.

When the child finally fell free of the straps, I clutched him to my chest, scooped the lady up over my shoulder, and managed to get my feet under me as I started wobbling away from the burning SUV. I had made it about sixty feet when the flames hit the gas tank. The whole thing went up in a giant ball of orange fire and black smoke.

Another passing motorist had stopped and snapped a picture with his cell phone, capturing me with the woman over one shoulder and the child clutched to my chest. The wrecked car and gigantic fireball behind me made the whole scene look like a promotional poster for a Rambo movie.

Fortunately, neither of them was seriously injured.

The wheels of fate had begun to turn. In a matter of hours, the local network TV affiliates had the pictures and the story, and they were lining up to interview me. Somehow, during the interviews, while I was trying to duck away from them starting to label me a hero, I got off onto, "This is just what any other regular American person would do in such a situation." Which morphed into what a great country we really had. And then into what was wrong with it and what needed to take place for us to regain control of our country. The networks picked that up immediately, and requests for interviews poured in from every media outlet in the country. I had changed from a regular guy who happened to own a pocketknife into the spokesman for John Q. Public on all matters, especially political.

I waited for all the insanity to subside and for my life to get back to normal again, but the increasing publicity started the ball rolling in a different direction. I was to find out later that all around the country, serious people were having serious conversations about who our country's next president should be.

At one point during the interviews, I had offered a list of the qualities that our next president should have in order to get us through the next four critical years of our country's existence.

The list was pretty darn simple, really. I thought our next president should be:

> ***Tough***
> ***Honest***
> ***Intelligent***
> ***Compassionate***
> ***Wary***

And he or she must have:

> ***Common sense***
> ***Integrity***
> ***Courage***
> ***Honor***
> ***Virtue***

It seemed that none of the popular candidates of either party possessed many, if any, of these qualities. They were all the typical professional-politician-type, who had long since lost all touch with the average American. And the average American knew it.

The serious people in the serious meetings liked my list, and they started looking for someone who actually *did* have those qualities.

Once they realized that all the name-brand politicians couldn't possibly have any of the qualities—they had been in the game too long and were completely controlled by special interests—the serious people started looking for a serious candidate outside of the political establishment. They started asking me to come and speak to their groups, to help identify and recruit a candidate with the qualities I had been talking about.

After searching for several months with no success, they were about to give up when the woman in charge of the actual marketing part of the campaign pointed to a big-screen TV at the back of a Chicago meeting room and said, "Guys, there is a man I can get elected." They all turned and looked at the television.

I was being interviewed about the wreck for what seemed like the millionth time. I had made my usual switch of topics—to avoid the hero discussion—to our country and what we needed in the way of leadership.

The serious people contacted me the next day and set up a meeting at Mike Shannon's Steaks and Seafood restaurant in St. Louis, for the following Tuesday. As I drove past Busch Stadium into downtown I had no idea what they had in mind. And if I had suspected what their intentions were, I wouldn't have gone.

After lunch, they broached the subject of my being a candidate for president. I thought this was tremendously funny, until I realized they were serious. At that point, I tried to come up with other potential candidates and good reasons why this was a truly ridiculous idea, while I started inching toward the door. But none of my arguments made any headway against their tide of optimism. They were convinced that I could represent the qualities we had been talking about.

Or maybe they were just tired of looking for someone.

It seemed that several of the potential candidates had some of the qualities they were looking for, but none had the quality they agreed was the most important one. They knew that in the next four years, America would face many critical challenges, from radical terrorists to powerful, greedy special-interest groups at home to, strangely enough, Congress itself, which had become its own special-interest group with no interest in—or feeling for—the average American citizen.

The quality they all agreed was the most important one, which was lacking in all the recognized candidates, was toughness. It was number one on the list

I had given them. I had previously described what the next president needed to be: "the toughest son of a bitch who ever walked through the front door the White House."

I had gone on to describe the ideal future president as ***"John Wayne with a really bad hangover,"*** which seemed to resonate with all of them. I don't know that I had the other characteristics they were looking for, but I guess I had enough of that one to make up for any other shortcomings. So, in short, they started the paperwork necessary to get my name on the ballot in the early primary states.

John Q. Public really must have had a bellyful of professional politicians, because in Philadelphia, on July 25, 2016, I was nominated as the party's official candidate—over a former president's wife—for the highest office in the land.

I had never actually agreed to run, but that became a moot point after everyone got caught up in the excitement of the campaign. People from all parts of the United States showed up to volunteer to do anything that would help reverse the course the country had been on for the last fifty years. The campaign sort of took on a life of its own, and I was not really an important part of it until the debates started.

I had been very apprehensive about the first debate because there had not been an opportunity for one in the primary, and I knew my opponent was more polished and informed than I was. For the first fifteen minutes, I was quiet as a mouse, totally engrossed in wishing I were somewhere else. Then the goofball called me a liar.

That brought about the clear distinction between a regular American guy and a politician. My mind went on autopilot as my body walked slowly across the stage and stopped six inches in front of his face. I didn't grab him, but I did put both hands on the top of his podium, lean over it, and tell him to retract that last statement, or else.

I hadn't really been listening to him, and I didn't know exactly why he had called me a liar, but it didn't matter. I wouldn't lie about anything, nor would I let anyone call me a liar. Millions of people saw the fear in his eyes and heard his voice quiver as he tried to respond. I instinctively tightened my jaw and told him one more time to retract his statement. He buckled and made a total mess of the rest of the debate.

We won the general election 59 percent to 41 percent against the brother of another former president, whose father was also a former president.

With 319 million people in this country, it seemed pretty unrealistic to voters that only two families in the entire country were qualified to fill the nation's top leadership position.

From that point on, it all became history.

OFFICE OF THE PRESIDENT OF THE UNITED STATES

———◆———

LIST OF THINGS TO DO

1. *Research actual powers of the office of president.*

2. *Fill vacant staff positions.*

3. *Read updated information on the leaders of China, Russia, India, and Iran.*

4. *Review tax code*

5. *Review latest revenue projections.*

6. *Prep for meeting with Chiefs of Staff.*

7. *Schedule first Cabinet meeting ASAP.*

CHAPTER TWO

NATIONAL SECURITY

———

"The only reason that we are able to sleep safely
at night is that there are rough men standing by
to wreak violence on those who would harm us."

— WINSTON CHURCHILL

AS THE MEMORIES FADED, MIKE'S voice became louder. The
Joint Chiefs were filing into the Oval Office. They had the demeanor of a high school principal entering a detention room full
of freshmen who'd been caught vandalizing the gym.

Well, okay then, let's just get this shit off on the right foot.

With a cold, hard voice, I said, "Good morning, gentlemen.
Be seated. I have a lot to talk about."

Mike shot me a warning glance that suggested I back off and
play nice, but it was too late for that. I had read their facial expressions and body language as they'd filed into the room, and I

knew these men had no respect for civilian politicians. Looking back at recent history that was probably with good reason.

I continued, "According to my reading of the Constitution, the president of the United States is also the commander-in-chief of its armed forces. Do we agree on that?"

Might as well get things straight from the get-go. No one said a word, but they all nodded their heads in agreement.

"Good," I said. "In that case, in the words of one of my personal heroes, Admiral Bull Halsey, when you're in command, command! Starting right this minute, that is what I intend to do.

"I would like to give you gentlemen a little understanding of exactly where I'm coming from. It is true that I've never served in the armed forces as such, and I am a civilian commander-in-chief. However, I did spend three and a half years in the army ROTC, and I learned a lot in the process. I enjoyed the military experience. I liked wearing the uniform. I liked the discipline, esprit de corps, chain of command, and philosophy of order and organization presented by the military way of life." I also really enjoyed firing all the weapons the army had at its disposal during summer camp.

"I understand that war is a continuum of politics by other means, and it is a necessary evil if we are to survive as a nation during these perilous times. I think it is important for you to entirely understand the tremendous amount of respect I have for you and the brave men and women in your command, and the thankfulness I have for your service to our country. I fully realize that each and every one of you and your families has endured many hardships as a result of your service to your country. It is my hope that we will form a relationship that enables us to accomplish whatever is necessary to ensure the safety and security of the citizens of our country."

Damn, that sounded good even to me.

"It is my desire to be a peacetime president and to focus this administration's efforts on the issues that make life better for the average American citizen. I intend to do the best job possible in the areas of jobs, the economy, and the environment, and to straighten up the current problems with our political structure. All of these issues are of great importance. However, they are completely meaningless unless we have a safe and secure country.

"Therefore, we're going to have to meet the challenge presented by terrorists, who are a clear and present danger to our country. I personally view these people as cowards, bullies, and crazy fanatics. They have no place in our world in the year 2017. I would like for us to negotiate, mediate, and civilize their thought processes, to eliminate the dangers they pose. But I realize this is impossible. These people are completely brainwashed at ages five to seven, and changing their minds is impossible.

"They are, in my mind, philosophically exactly the same as rattlesnakes. Being a country boy, I know exactly how to handle rattlesnakes. You either leave them alone, or you kill them. They're not going to change their minds, and you're not going to modernize their philosophies. We are not going to change them into good little snakes. Sadly, there are no choices but to leave them alone or kill them.

"That being said, our job breaks into two separate activities: find them, kill them. It appears to me that our intelligence agencies have responsibility for the first part of the equation, and you gentlemen have responsibility for the second part. The main thing I want to accomplish today is to get your input on the first part, so we all leave here today with a clear understanding of our capabilities when it comes to finding them.

"I have read the briefings, and I have a basic understanding of our intelligence apparatus, but not a working knowledge. This being my first day in office, I look to you gentlemen as the only people I know at this point whom I can respect and trust, and I value your opinion. I would appreciate a rundown on our intelligence apparatus capabilities, starting with your own intelligence units.

"Do your people work in complete harmony with each other and with the national intelligence agencies?"

When I looked into the eyes of each chief during the ensuing minute of total shocked silence, I knew I had started out on the right foot. This was a lot more of a down-to-earth and get-to-the-point meeting than they had expected. They were not ready to jump in bed with me yet, but the arrogant, sarcastic looks had left their faces and been replaced with a wonderful look of, *what in the hell have we gotten ourselves into now?*

Over the course of the next three hours of intense discussions—on the state of readiness of the intelligence apparatus and our military capabilities—an initial mutual respect began to develop. I hoped it would increase, and become more productive, for the next four years.

At least I had given them an opportunity to see how my mental furniture was arranged.

The Chiefs were intelligent, honest, and capable. As they left, I shook hands with them, looked them straight in the eye, thanked them again for their service to our country, and expressed the hope that we could work together to bring our beloved country out of the shadow of terrorism. It was easy to tell that they were a completely different group of guys than the ones who had arrogantly walked into the office hours earlier.

Aretha Franklin was right. *R.E.S.P.E.C.T.*

They were also going to be a lot busier than they had previously been. I had given them explicit orders to return to the office in exactly seventy-two hours, armed with complete battle plans for the top ten most likely terrorist attack scenarios.

One half-day down, 2,917 to go.

Mike had been sitting quietly to the side of the antique oval table we'd been gathered around. Come to think of it, he had not said one word during the entire meeting—the longest period of time he'd gone speechless since he was two years old, I imagined. After the door closed, he held his hand on the knob and looked at me as though he had never seen me before.

"I've known you for forty years, and I can't believe that was you doing the talking for the last three hours."

"Good or bad?" I asked.

"Not sure, but it sure as hell was impressive," he replied.

"Well, they say the common man can rise to the position. Look at Harry Truman. He certainly did, and so can I. Now, where in the hell is the lunchroom? That little meeting just worked up an appetite for me."

"Beats me," the smartest man I know replied.

"Have you got a map of this place? I don't want to spend the next four years trying to find all the bathrooms around here," said the most powerful man in the world.

Seventy-two hours later, the Joint Chiefs were back with their preliminary battle plans. In the meantime, I had gained a great deal of information on our intelligence systems from several direct inquiries to the intelligence community.

Over the past two-plus years, the vivid media descriptions and videos of suicide bombings, beheadings, and victims being burned alive had awakened people worldwide to the insanity and viciousness of terrorist groups, and I think my rattlesnake speech to the Chiefs had brought them to the understanding that there would be no more Mr. Nice Guy activities in our war on terror.

At the beginning of the terrorists' savage onslaught, they had been too few in number and too widely scattered to be decent targets of our offensive weapons, but now they occupied large chunks of geography and presented much more worthwhile targets. Now was the time for the discussion.

"Do you gentlemen believe that it would be in our best interest to wait until we are attacked yet again by these people, or should we consider preemptive strikes?"

Their response was immediate and unanimous.

"They have slapped our face enough times already, Mr. President," was one admiral's observation.

"Very well, gentlemen. I concur. Are any of you gentlemen opposed, in any way, to the use of nuclear weapons at this point in time?"

The room turned deadly silent as they looked first at each other, and then back at me.

"Under what conditions?" asked the admiral.

"Massive worldwide preemptive strikes at our best seven hundred targets," was my immediate response. "Seven days of round-the-clock bombing, including the use of nuclear weapons on key targets. By using US Air Force bombers and the Navy's ballistic missile cruisers, I want to deliver a knockout punch that they will not recover from in our lifetime. As I said before, they are rattlesnakes. Either leave them alone or kill them."

I could tell that they realized I was dead serious. The time had finally come for the discussion they'd never wanted to have.

During the period after the accident, when I was trying to duck the fifteen-seconds-of-fame conversation, I had come up with a list of all the things that made our country the wonderful place it was, and a list of the problems we faced as a nation.

The conversation had then expanded into a formalized list of the things that needed to be fixed:

Terrorism
The economy
Congressional term limits
Campaign finance
Health care
Immigration policies
The environment
Our aging infrastructure
Foreign relations
The judicial system
Illegal drugs

And, last but definitely not least, our political system itself.

I had no special knowledge of any of those topics, but like many other American citizens, I did watch the news at night, and I saw what was going on around me. I related those occurrences to my own role as an average American citizen.

What I saw and heard on the nightly news always kind of made me want to throw up.

It was obvious that we the people were constantly being raped by big business and lied to by our leaders. We were becoming less important to everyone in general, as the powers of the special-interest groups grew exponentially and the threats of terrorist attacks at home increased daily.

This had been, of course, a big topic of conversation at bars, restaurants, and social clubs like our Elks Lodge back home. But no one had done anything about it.

Not until now, my friend.

OFFICE OF THE PRESIDENT OF THE UNITED STATES

———

LIST OF THINGS TO DO

1. *Get better intel on terrorist activities.*

2. *Memorize military stats.*

3. *Research treaties and agreements with allies.*

4. *Schedule meetings with allied leaders.*

5. *Have Mike transition campaign structure into political action groups.*

6. *Research Department of Defense contracts.*

7. *Remove all troops from current combat areas.*

8. *Modernize all combat units.*

9. *Reorganize the Veterans Administration.*

CHAPTER THREE

IT'S THE ECONOMY, STUPID

———

"We have the best government that money can buy."

— ANONYMOUS

IN THE SIMPLE AND SUCCINCT words of the "greatest Cajun mind of our time," it is all about the economy.

James Carville of Slidell, Louisiana, is Cajun by birth, a Democrat by choice, and a sage by nature. In spite of looking a lot like Yoda and being married to a big-time Republican strategist, he is the kind of guy people feel good listening to whenever he starts talking about important issues in his famous rolling Cajun accent. He is the one who coined the phrase, "It's the economy, stupid." Thanks, James.

Our rich and powerful nation is broke.   End of story.

Our national debt is more than eighteen trillion dollars, however in the hell much that is. And our highly intelligent leaders were gleefully spending more than the government was taking in every day, thereby going further into debt on a daily basis.

In some cases, debt could be a useful tool for funding necessities or investments. Most of us everyday citizens needed to borrow money to finance large purchases like cars, education, and a family home. No problem, as long as you had the one big qualification that all honest lending institutions looked for: the ability to repay the loan. If you didn't have the income to make the payments, you shouldn't get the loan. Plus, any financial expert worth his or her salt would advise you to borrow money only for large investment-type purchases, not for everyday expenses or luxuries.

So what had the geniuses in charge of the finances of the richest country on the planet (that is, Congress) been doing with OUR money? They had been spending it as though it were water and there were no tomorrow. They couldn't care less that the point of no return, of not ever being able to pay it back, was fast approaching.

The total economic picture consisted of several categories. Government spending and taxation were of great concern to all Americans, because we were personally affected by them. Next came the matter of jobs and opportunities for all Americans to be gainfully employed. High finance included banks, the stock market, and all the financial institutions, which played a big important part in the overall economy. Too big to fail my ass.

All of these things worked together to improve or hurt our total economic picture.

Two hours after the election results were official, I had asked one of my new transition team members to get us a paper copy of the federal budget. Twenty-four hours later, it had arrived at our new Washington transition office in the form of a tidy little three-foot-thick book. Since that time, I'd spent several hours a day going through the budget, taking the dollar figures out of each line item and inserting them into my own three-column spreadsheet, under the headings "Item," "Necessity," and "Luxury."

When I had finished that down-and-dirty preliminary look at the budget, it was obvious that over 50 percent of the federal government's so-called discretionary spending could easily be labeled luxuries. The purchases would have been called that if they were in an average family's budget.

"So, Mike, we make big cuts in the federal budget and start paying off the national debt as fast as possible," I explained to my chief of staff.

"Congress will never let you do anything like that."

"That is what the people elected us to this office to do, Mike, and we have to do it. I know Congress is going to go straight through the dome of the Capitol building, but that's what must be done, and that's what we're going to do.

Our forefathers did a tremendous job of starting this country out on the right foot, especially by

establishing the three branches of government that supposedly balance each other. But almost since its inception, and certainly for the last fifty years, Congress has been steadily usurping the power of the presidency—when they're not busy feathering their own nests.

"It is their job to pass laws regulating the societal issues we face every day, not to run the country on a day-to-day basis. It is the job of the executive branch to be the CEO of the country and to attend to the day-to-day administration of the government. That is going to be the biggest challenge we face in this administration, and that's one fight we have to win, or we will never accomplish anything else."

"Yeah, good freaking luck with that one," Mike said with an exasperated tone I had heard many times before. "Congress has steadily increased its power for the last seventy-five years, and it intends to do so into the future. There is no way you are going to be able to stop them and get the power the presidency should have back down Pennsylvania Avenue to the White House."

"You're absolutely right, Mike. I can't do that. But the American people can, and the American people are going to have to step up if we are to have the slightest chance of preventing this country from going down the drain in the next four years.

"We are going to have to educate the American people about the fact that in a democracy, they are the

ones who actually have the power. They are the ones who hire and fire the politicians, so they will have to be the ones to start the petitions that drag these dinosaurs out of the hallowed halls of Congress. They will need to find some new blood that is not owned and operated by special interests. That is the only way to take this government from the greedy folks and give it back to the people. And if we don't start with the national debt, the rest will be immaterial."

I had grown up poor. My parents had lost everything in the Great Depression, including their hopes, dreams, and ambitions. They had to be focused on survival, and they would remain so all their lives. The acute lack of money left a lasting impression on their lives and had made a tremendous impact on mine, too. This gave me a distinct advantage over any Washington insider. Nobody had to explain being poor to me. I knew from firsthand experience what it felt like to wear worn-out clothes and live on the wrong side of town, and I knew what those feelings did to a person.

Many people had wondered what would happen if the government went bankrupt. The impact of our government's inability to pay its employees—such as those in the military and law enforcement—would have been devastating and would have resulted in anarchy. The government's answer would be to crank up the presses and start printing more money, which would cause rampant inflation and make the situation even worse for average Americans. What money they did have would become virtually worthless.

Many books had been written on the terrible potential effects of the United States' going bankrupt. But none of them had ever been able to convey the sickening ordeal that the American people would face in that situation, all brought on by the terrible greed of some individuals and the stupidity of our elected officials.

Even though none of us liked big government, we all understood that without the services provided by the federal government, our society would turn into chaos in short order. This would leave a void in control and leadership, which would immediately be filled not only by the ruthless and greedy people, but also by dangerous people with no regard for human life. There were many scenarios of what would happen if our country went bankrupt—lots of different versions of bad, none good.

The answer to this big complex debt problem was actually pretty darn simple. Treat it just like your own budget at home, only with more zeros. Reduce your spending and make sure your income covers your expenses. Common sense is a real thing.

Reducing federal expenditures was actually a pretty simple thing to do with some common sense, which I had been using since I started dividing the federal budget into luxuries and necessities. The first savings came in a big chunk called foreign aid. It was found under several categories in the budget, including the Department of Defense, Department of Agriculture, Department of State, and a few other departments. It all boiled down to one philosophy: you don't borrow money and then try to buy friends with it.

Yep, definitely not necessary.

Without wasting time consulting with Congress, I sent a letter to every country we had been giving money to, thanking them for their friendship and explaining that the taxpayers of the United States could no longer afford to give money away.

Some of the countries were very understanding and continued to be our friends and allies. Others screamed to the high heavens and even admitted that they never liked us in the first place. Congress went completely crazy and pretty much admitted that these other countries would not be friendly toward us unless they were receiving a large chunk of our taxpayers' hard-earned money.

Interestingly enough, we never received even one disparaging comment from the American taxpayers.

The next large chunk of tax dollars to be rescued from the hands of the bought-and-paid-for politicians came in the form of the Farm Bill.

In 1933, the Great Depression combined with record crop yields threatened to wipe out the family farmer, so Congress, in its infinite wisdom, passed the first Farm Bill, designed to save the small family farm.

It actually wiped out the family farmer even more efficiently than the depression would have, and it put all the pieces in place so that the developing entity known as Big Ag could steal billions of taxpayer dollars. Big Ag comprised the giant corporations that came to completely control agriculture in our country.

Since the passing of the first Farm Bill, Big Ag had gained a monopoly on the food supply. It owned giant chunks of the farming land in our country. They owned the vast majority of the resources that produced beef, pork, poultry, corn, wheat, soybeans, and all the byproducts and processed foods associated with those commodities. They had purchased millions of acres of farmland, grain-handling facilities, and food-processing factories, using taxpayers' money given to them by Congress.

All honest business, and especially farming, works best with the least amount of government intervention, because with government intervention comes a silent partner: special-interest groups.

These companies had more lobbyists on their payrolls than cowboys and tractor drivers, and they completely controlled the price and quality of every slice of bread and strip of bacon you'd eaten in the last twenty-plus years. They had removed the family farm from the landscape, much in the same fashion that European settlers had cleaned out the Native Americans. Good old Manifest Destiny at work again.

We'd all heard of farmers getting paid not to grow anything, at the same time that we were hearing about dramatically increasing crop yields and our ability to feed the rest of the world. All of this as millions of people around the globe were starving. A little common sense was definitely needed here.

So we did the same thing with this issue that we had done with the foreign aid problem. I again sent a letter to all concerned and stopped all farm subsidy payments to recipients who had a gross income of more than $750,000 a year. Yep, Big Ag and Congress squalled like mashed cats. The taxpayers loved it!

———◆———

Off we went, Mike, six accountants, two lawyers, and yours truly, page by page through the budget, making lists of necessities and luxuries. It was a fascinating lesson in corruption and greed. I envisioned the process of how these taxpayers' dollars had ended up going into the pockets of the fat cats. I could almost smell the cigar smoke in the back rooms of the Capitol building, see the shadowy deals being made, and hear the laughter of the politicians and lobbyists who thought it was funny that the taxpayers would be paying for monstrosities.

After three hundred hours of diligent budget-reading, our country had a completely balanced budget for only the twelfth time in the last seventy-seven years. It included a debit reduction plan that would totally eliminate our national debt in nineteen years and seven months.

Was Congress going to be happy with it? Boy, howdy.

Having come up with solutions to the national debt and the budget deficit, we then jumped right into the next facet of the economy: jobs. None of the economic principles work unless we have a fully engaged workforce. Not to mention that a good job is the pride and soul of the average American, who made this nation great in the first place.

We split the problem of joblessness into three sections: unemployment, underemployment, and unwillingness to work.

For the unemployed, by executive order, we established a strict tariff policy. If a foreign country sold one hundred dollars' worth of goods to the United States, they would also have to buy one hundred dollars' worth of goods from the United States. It's called balance of trade. It levels the playing field, and it works every time.

We then, again by executive order, decreed that the federal government itself would buy no products or services from any persons, firms, or corporations unless they were headquartered in, and paid taxes to, the United States. All members of their boards of directors and their top management people had to be US citizens.

It stands to reason that if we make the things here and we buy them here, we should be able to provide

employment for our own citizens—so they can afford to buy the things they make.

That should make Walmart, Halliburton, and several hundred other companies ecstatic. You betcha!

We then revived and improved the old Department of Employment Security, which had found private industry jobs for millions of people from the Great Depression up to the 1980s. It was, very simply, a computerized clearinghouse where people looking for jobs could go to find out what jobs were available anywhere in the country. It also gave businesses help with locating qualified employees. We found that it could easily be funded by eliminating a few small luxuries from the federal budget, like the congressional sauna, limo service, and barbershop. Really!

The next step in eliminating unemployment was to provide prospective employees with appropriate skill sets. So we set up a blue-chip committee that would study the issue of training people who were looking for jobs. The committee would take a good look at what skills businesses needed and how to provide, effectively and efficiently, the required training to prospective job applicants. It was a small committee of only thirty people, representing the fields of industry, labor, and education. They, like all members of our volunteer focus work groups, had a thirty-day deadline, by which they would bring us back the information we needed to solve the problem.

Every day lasts a long time when you don't have an income, so it was my goal to get as many people working as soon as possible.

For the underemployed, we set up another task force of knowledgeable individuals, who would determine what the jobs of the near future would be and establish proper training and education facilities for those needed to work up into those positions. The costs of the program would be shared by the industries that would hire the graduates and the educational institutions selling the services.

I had heard too many stories from parents whose children had worked very hard to get a college degree, only to come home and live in their old rooms while waiting to hear about a possible job opening at the local McDonald's. Too much time, effort, and money had gone into educating these bright young minds for them not to be able to secure decent jobs in their chosen fields upon graduation.

We needed a consolidated effort from the business and education communities to identify the jobs of the future and prepare our young people to fill those jobs. We split this effort into two groups, based on the wishes of the young folks when they graduated from high school. Some kids couldn't wait to further their education in college, and others were no longer interested in sitting in classrooms. They wanted to get out into the big, brave world.

We established another blue-ribbon committee to determine how we could set up a world-class system of technical and community colleges, to prepare young people for rewarding, well-paying jobs if they chose not to go the four-year university route. The committee was also charged with finding ways to reduce the cost of a college education by 50 percent and establishing resource centers for students to obtain zero-interest loans.

For the "don't want to work" category, we established a program of national service that was closely akin to the old CCC and WPA programs of the Great Depression. Our infrastructure was becoming obsolete and in bad shape, and it could really use the labor-intensive help that able-bodied men and women could provide while learning a trade.

If you were not physically or mentally handicapped, and you were able to work but unable to find a job anywhere else, you could enter into one of the many units of this program, the main goals of which were to maintain and improve our infrastructure, public lands, and buildings and tear down and rebuild the ghettos in all the large cities of our country. The program was accompanied by a 20-percent-per-year reduction in welfare and all other social entitlement programs enrolled in by able-bodied people. This made a lot more money available for those who really needed it, and it helped to reduce overall federal expenditures.

During the discussions that led to the solutions to these problems, the topic of people from all around the world being in this country illegally, and taking up a good chunk of the national paycheck, naturally came up. This resulted in another executive order, proclaiming that to have a job in the United States, you must be a taxpaying, legal citizen of the United States. The penalty for violating this order was born by employers who had hired illegal employees, and it was ten times the amount of the illegal payroll the employer had paid.

That should make a whole lot of employers appreciate citizenship.

Yes, sir!

One of the most interesting facts uncovered during our research was that CEOs for some of the fast-food chains made between $10,000 and $15,000 an hour, while their employees made $7.50 an hour. I understood completely that some folks should make more money than others based on their education, experience, and worth to their employers, but that difference seemed a bit extreme to me.

The millions in bonuses paid to CEOs—which had caused the crash in 2008—were even more unconscionable.

If all the solutions to our economic problems were to work, and to really have a workable plan, we were going to have to do one more bit of financial adjustment on the revenue side.

Within the next two weeks, I was going to issue a challenge to Congress to finally insert some common sense into the taxation of our citizens—including corporations, whom the courts had decided were actually citizens. Really? Did they have birth certificates? Did they have children they needed to put through college?

The paperwork going to Congress would call for the immediate revocation of all federal tax regulations, which would be replaced by one simple, solitary tax regulation: every person, firm, and corporation in the country would be required to pay 9.87 percent of his, her, or its gross annual income. No withholdings, no deductions, no breaks for fat cats. Just the straight percent of gross income that would be needed to fully fund our government's necessary expenses. Anyone making less than $15,000 a year was exempt from paying. According to a panel of the sharpest actuaries we could find, this was the only actual way to equalize the tax burden across the board for all strata of Americans.

The chances of congressional approval for this very necessary item were considerably less than zero.

That wasn't a problem, however, because this was going to be clearly and honestly explained to the citizens, taxpayers, and voters of this country by yours truly. I would explain it during a series of televised appeals, which would ask our citizens to contact their representatives and senators and absolutely demand that they support these measures wholeheartedly—or they would face an immediate and ugly response from their constituents. And (thank you, Mike) there were very capable bipartisan organizations all across America prepared to start making calls.

The only category still left to address to improve the economy concerned the financial community itself. I established one more blue-ribbon committee, this time of unbiased experts in the financial community. The very capable vice president, who had extensive knowledge and experience in the field, headed up this committee. My charge to the committee was to recommend any and all steps necessary to keep banks, mortgage companies, the stock market, and any and all other financial institutions from running amok and doing the stupid things they'd been doing in the name of greed—which had caused recessions, depressions, and significant financial downturns.

At the end of the initial meeting, I scheduled the next meeting to be held in two weeks. If you are in financial trouble, you need help now, not next year.

It began to seem that we were spending all of our time establishing committees, instead of actually fixing problems. I mentioned this to Mike after a morning staff meeting, and he loosened his tie, smiled his very best happy smile, and said, "I've been trying to figure out if you were doing this on purpose, or if it was just coming about in a natural progression."

"You're starting to scare me again, Mike. What do you see that I don't?"

His smile turned into a laugh as he leaned back in his chair and tugged at his sideburns, which he always did when he was immersed in his deepest thoughts.

"Well, you've just fixed the one of the biggest problems this country is facing. In the past, 99 percent of input into this government had come from lobbyists for special-interest groups, who had convinced Congress that something needed to be done to improve the country. But what they actually wanted was to get their paws on more taxpayer money. So Congress would then pass a law that did very little, if any, good for the taxpayers, although it helped the rich get much richer. And you are fixing it with an influx of honest information into 'Disneyland on the Potomac.'

"What we have now is a basic change in input. Committees of experts with the good of the country—instead of a profit motive—in mind provide good new ideas to the executive branch, which in turn assigns these ideas to a federal agency that reports to the president, not to Congress. This takes Congress, lobbyists, and the fat cats completely out of the input system, purifying and streamlining the process. The executive branch is effectively put in charge of daily operations, which is exactly the way the founding fathers envisioned it. The president is now in a position of playing offense instead of defense, and you only gain ground when you're on the offense."

During my inaugural address and every public appearance since, I had asked for input and creative ideas from all Americans. We had developed an ultra-modern email, text, and phone system to receive and handle the responses. The thousands of ideas we'd gotten from everyday citizens concerning how to improve the country had been nothing short of awesome. They were responsible for several hundred new innovations.

OFFICE OF THE PRESIDENT OF THE UNITED STATES

LIST OF THINGS TO DO

1. Motivate all financial regulators and get them into high gear.

2. Position VP as head of all financial regulation.

3. Engage legal staff in financial areas and create new tax structure.

4. Meet with tax actuaries and legal staff.

5. Review foreign aid, Farm Bill, and all other savings measures.

6. Meet with secretaries of agriculture and state.

7. Reduce student loans to one percent.

8. Double the size and scope of the Small Business Administration

CHAPTER FOUR

CONGRESS

———— ✦ ————

"Reader, suppose you are an idiot. And suppose you
are a member of Congress. But I repeat myself."

— MARK TWAIN

MIKE HAD TAKEN THE LEAD on making all the fact-finding activities fall into place and making sure the right people were in
the right rooms at the right time. His ability to find and motivate extremely knowledgeable people was phenomenal, and we
were off on the right foot in an amazingly short amount of time.

"Mike, you have done more good for this country in just
forty days than most presidents have done in four years in office, and I appreciate it," I said one morning over the first cup of
coffee of the day.

"Wait a couple of days until the pushback starts," Mike replied. "It'll come from Congress and the fat cats we've just cas-
trated. You won't be so happy when they start shooting at us."

"We don't have time to wait, Mike. Let's start the organizational groundwork for the public opinion campaigns today. We know which senators and representatives are the most bought and paid for, and which ones will scream the first and loudest. Contact your people in each of their home states, and get them activated to fire up the electorate."

Article I of the Constitution of the first Continental Congress, held on July 4, 1776, gave us the original structure and duties of Congress.

Today's Congress was made up of 100 senators, two from each state, and 435 representatives. ***The will of the people of our great country had therefore been funneled down from 319 million to 535 people, of which only about 15 actually held all the power.***

"Mike, how many lobbyists did you say there are in Washington, DC?"

"18,267" was his immediate response.

"So in actuality, 15 people—bought and paid for by special-interest groups with the encouragement, or discouragement, of 18,267 lobbyists—make the laws that 319 million people have to abide by every day?"

"Your tax dollars at work, Mr. President."

"Mike, in 1971 it cost seventy thousand dollars to get elected as a US representative every two years. Today, it costs over a million dollars for a representative and more than six million for a six-year senatorial term. This is a problem in the system that has to be fixed, pronto."

Mike looked at me with that menacing look he does so well and said, "Did you know that over half the members of Congress are millionaires, and 85 percent of them are lawyers? And they have a 13 percent approval rating and a 95 percent reelection rate."

"Well, there you have it! That's one thing that needs to be fixed immediately, if not sooner."

We had known from day one that the president did not have the authority to initiate all the changes necessary to get the country headed in the right direction again. But we also understood that the president has the opportunity and the duty to motivate the American people to exercise all rights given to them by the Constitution. Not only did voters elect their leaders in Congress, but they had the right and responsibility to take those people to task when they failed to adequately represent the desires of their constituents.

In the last days of our first year in office, the game plan became one in which the president would identify a problem and institute or propose a remedy, which would immediately draw the wrath of some special-interest group—who would then scream at their bought-and-paid-for congressional officeholder, who would summon the press corps and alert them to the fact that the president was trying to destroy the country.

We would then have the he-said-she-said standoff that had crippled our country's ability to respond to the problems threatening our future. The bought-and-paid-for politicos were not in any position to be telling the truth about what was actually good for the country.

The only answer to this situation was to have the congressperson in question spoken to directly by his or her constituents. These conversations needed to be carried out quickly and decisively through a flood of phone calls, texts, and emails from the public; these messages would be the direct result of an honest and simple explanation of the facts by the president of the United States.

This would shed the light of truth on the situation—and on the poor congressperson, who would then be caught in a position where he or she could no longer serve two masters. At that point, Congress would have to go along with either the constituents who had elected them or the special interests that had purchased their services, along with their souls. Not a good place to be in.

Our founding fathers had been serious about a government by the people, of the people, and for the people. Several important issues had been included in the first drafts of the Constitution, only to be left out as it progressed to the final version we live by today. The first drafts had included provisions that were specifically designed to ensure the adherence of elected officials to the desires of their constituents. They had included term limits and recall provisions, and they had prohibited any kind of influence-peddling. They also had balanced budget requirements. Should elected officials become forgetful of who their boss really was, they could lose their jobs quickly, if demanded by an astute and aggrieved pack of angry voters demanding the respect they deserve.

The ugly truth was that senators and representatives were not accountable to those they represented, except on Election Day.

———

Early the next morning, a hard, driving rain hammered against my office windows as Mike and Daniel, his bright assistant, squished across the floor carrying several volumes of information on the current status of the US Congress.

Mike asked, "Mr. President, you know how much the Speaker of the House makes?"

"No, Mike, I really don't."

"His base salary is $223,500 a year, and when he leaves office he gets $1 million in office expenses a year for five years, in addition to his retirement. His base salary alone is 600 percent more than the average American wage-earner gets, and they sure as hell don't get a million a year after they leave their job."

Daniel got fired up and chimed in, "The average American worker also does not get a free gym, complete with a swimming pool and sauna, and free parking at both Dulles and Reagan airports."

My chief of staff started showing his Irish heritage by pointing his finger at me as he explained, "Congressional pay starts at $174,000 a year, which is in the top 8 percent of all income-earners in America today. Representatives average $1,350,000 per year in office expenses, and senators average $2,300,000 a year, with the highest expense allowance for a senator being $4.69 million a year. They also get, in addition to the other perks Daniel just mentioned, limo service when they're in Washington, health care subsidies, free travel anywhere they want to go, and, oh yeah, they get 239 days a year off, because they're usually only in session about 126 days a year."

I was totally amazed. "I heard Nancy Pelosi say, not too long ago, that Congress lives paycheck to paycheck," I replied. "But I just found out that she's worth $58 million, so I guess she won't starve. I also heard Representative Jim Moran say legislators can't afford to live decently. I wonder how he thinks the rest of the people in this country live."

Mike said, "All of this, Mr. President, is what they get from the taxpayers. You want to talk about the under-the-table money they get from the fat cats they really work for?"

"No Mike, I just had my blueberry muffin, and I don't want to puke it up on the carpet."

The real problem with the way Congress works is that of the 535 elected office-holders, only about 15 have any real power. They elect their own congressional leaders, who are completely controlled by special-interest groups that have only their own interests at heart.

The Supreme Court has ruled that recall petitions, which enabled citizens to take the office away from crooked or incompetent federal elected officials, are unconstitutional. Congress itself passed several laws that allowed for unlimited campaign contributions by unnamed individuals and organizations. Unnamed? Really?

And that, my friend, is how we, the American people, lost control of our country.

And that, my friend, is how we, the American people, lost control of our country.

And that, my friend, is how we, the American people, lost control of our country.

Much of our campaign had been built around the fact that Congress was pretty well a giant mess, and we intended to improve that situation if elected.

In many meetings with senior staff, and especially with our four legislative liaison people, we discussed the possibility of identifying honest, like-minded congressmen and women with whom we could work.

I knew there had to be more gifted, honest, and courageous people in Congress than just Senator Elizabeth Warren. After three months of investigating this possibility, we identified nine senators and thirty-one representatives who had not been bought off yet, and who actually had the best interests of their constituents at heart.

I wanted to develop a relationship with these people as soon as possible, so I invited them and their families to an informal, old-fashioned barbecue on the White House lawn. The weather turned out to be perfect, and the ribs and baked beans were awesome. I spent most of my time talking to the spouses and children, and I let our liaison staff spend quality time with the members of Congress. My only instructions were to keep it social and not discuss any business.

Air hockey was one of my few sports-oriented passions. The only piece of furniture I had brought to Washington, DC, with me was my air hockey table. I had played a lot at home, and I was pretty good with the puck and paddles. I started by beating a few of the smaller kids, and I worked my way up to the teen-agers without losing a game. Eventually even some of the adults gave it a try. I beat them, too.

This was a good start toward establishing myself as a regular guy instead of the unapproachable holder of our highest office.

After the new wore off air hockey and my arm got tired, I brought out my old Fender and started playing a little music. It had never been disclosed during the campaign that I was a guitar player, and everyone was totally amazed at how really awful I sounded. After two songs, I gave the guitar to a representative's wife who was a wonderful guitarist. She played several songs and completely swept everyone away. When she handed the guitar back to me, I autographed it with a felt-tip pen and gave it back to her, saying, "It would be criminal for me to play it again after the beautiful performance you've just given."

My next job was to hand-crank a giant ice cream machine, which I did while telling humorous stories of life back home. They all loved my down-to-earth approach and were completely enjoying the day, when I started dishing out the best homemade peach ice cream they had ever tasted.

One of the young bucks in the opposition party, who had previously commented on my ultraconservative approach to the White House budget, asked if this little soirée had put a kink in the White House monthly food budget. I told him no; I had paid out of my own pocket. He looked at me and then laughed, and I look back at him and didn't laugh.

After an uneasy silence, I said, "Today cost me $1,281.67, and I thought it was worth every penny of it." He looked at me for a minute totally speechless, and then a little look of respect crossed his face.

I guess in the town that greed built, people are more used to receiving freebies than paying for their own fun.

As they left, everyone shook hands with me and thanked me. I knew I hadn't bought any votes, but I was absolutely sure that we had begun some alliances based on mutual respect.

In the following days, word about our little picnic spread, and my liaison staff was much better received under the dome. Several other senators and representatives wanted to know when they might be invited to such an occasion.

Three weeks later, the forty officeholders who had attended the BBQ were invited to an official state dinner honoring the president of France, as were their husbands and wives. I didn't know about the guys, but that pretty well sold the ladies on the fact that maybe the president had some diplomatic qualities after all.

There is also a darker side to politics in DC.

Our first big vote in Congress was on a bill that was critical to our efforts in reducing the national debt. It had squeaked by the House by a narrow margin and was tied fifty to fifty in the Senate. The legislative liaison staff had worked tirelessly to get to this point—we'd had an intense strategy session the afternoon before it was to be voted on—but they could do no more. Everyone counted it as our first big loss.

Many years before, Mike had taught me that it was a great idea to keep a little black book of favors both received and given, and of other miscellaneous information that could become useful in the future. I looked at a couple of pages in my little black book. Something I came across gave me hope. Maybe we had a chance.

One of the senators who had spoken long and loud against the bill had always run on the platform of family values. My book had the name of his mistress on page thirty-seven.

That night, one of my spotters in the Capitol let me know that the good gentleman was still in his office at 10:20 p.m. I immediately made a clandestine trip up Pennsylvania Avenue and walked into his office.

He looked up from the book he was reading and said, "Good evening, Mr. President."

He wasn't going to stand up, so I said, "Keep your seat, Senator. This is just a social call." He looked back down and continued reading his book as I discussed the weather for two minutes.

I then leaned across his desk and quietly said, "Senator, I need your vote tomorrow, and if I don't get it, Judy's picture is going to be on the front page of *The Washington Post*." He showed no emotion and just kept reading his book.

After a few minutes, he said, without even looking up, "You have my vote."

I quietly said, "Thank you, Senator," and gently closed the door as I left.

The next morning, when I turned on the TV news, there he was, front and center in a sharp new suit. He was explaining that he had changed his mind on the issue, and that even though he did not like me or my philosophies, he was honor-bound to vote for the bill, because it was in the best interest of the nation's citizens.

I have often said that I don't like political games. Never said I didn't know how to play them.

OFFICE OF THE PRESIDENT OF THE UNITED STATES

———

LIST OF THINGS TO DO

1. *Schedule meeting with constitutional convention group.*

2. *Assign three members of legal staff to constitutional convention research.*

3. *Quiet heads up to forty congressional members re: constitutional convention.*

4. *Finesse media discussion re: constitutional convention.*

5. *Make personal trip to Wall Street.*

CHAPTER FIVE

THE DREAM TEAM

———

"You can't make good decisions
based on bad information."

— ALBERT EINSTEIN

I HAD ALWAYS BEEN BIG on watching TV news, reading newspapers, and gaining information from knowledgeable people. It seemed, however, that when you passed the Washington, DC, city limits, you automatically went into a sort of twilight zone, where information became distorted and the only facts and figures came from people with a selfish interest in having certain specific information put in front of you. The public relations people called this putting a spin on an issue. I called it putting spit on the truth, and I called the people doing it whores, because they had sold their souls.

There was no shortage of information, but there was a tremendous question about the validity of any of it. This made my job somewhere between extremely difficult and impossible.

Twenty-some years ago, I had been picked by the governor of my home state to start a program to fix a specific problem. I was unofficially the recognized leader in the field in my state, and I was very excited to have the opportunity to put in place the program that would fix the problem. I was to have a staff of seventeen, of my choosing. The main requirement was that these people needed to have the ability to come up with new ideas to fix an old problem. As I mentally waded through the fifty or sixty names that came to mind, I could not think of a single person who was going to do any out-of-the-box thinking.

The problem was not going to go away by serving up old ideas to fix old problems. So I journeyed to a small four-year college where bright young kids who had to work their way through school. In eight days, I had hired seventeen of the most intelligent young people I had ever met. None of them had the slightest idea of what the problem was or how to fix it, but they knew how to think outside of the proverbial box.

I gave up the executive office space that my new agency had been issued, and we held court in a fairly small meeting room, around a large table that was reminiscent of King Arthur's Round Table. I explained the problem from its beginnings, all the statistics that defined it, and all its social and economic implications.

After thirty days of learning, researching, and brainstorming, they—having named themselves the Dream Team—had come up with some astounding solutions. We all went into private industry and applied the principles we had developed. The results were phenomenal, our solutions worked perfectly, and the business leaders and politicians were ecstatic.

———

Early on a Monday morning, I found Mike working his way through the row of offices next to the Oval Office, spreading a bit of cheer to the secretaries who hated Monday mornings. I offered him one of my cherished blueberry muffins and said, "Mike, I've got an idea."

"Um hum," said my always-optimistic chief of staff.

"Are you getting any straight-up, honest information from anyone around here?"

"Mr. President, they are only telling us what is in their own best interest. That includes damn near everyone on our own staff."

"Exactly, Michael! That's my point exactly." I told him the story of the Dream Team, and I had him fire up our accounting guru and find enough money and open positions in the executive department budget to hire twelve of the sharpest young people in our country. This in itself turned out to be a large problem, but we did some creative thinking and came up with the money—and the twelve open positions. There had never been any positions alloted for a Dream Team, but I had always believed that creativeness is an important part of leadership.

We put out a nationwide search at universities, asking for their most creative recent graduates. We were rewarded with thousands of applications. We had the senior staff whittle those down to four applicants for each position. The staff conducted phone interviews, and then Mike personally interviewed the two finalists for each position.

In the meeting room down the hall from the Oval Office, the twelve new employees had pastries and excellent coffee, and then they got an impassioned one-hour explanation from the president of the United States himself of how important this project was, and how the very future of the country was at stake.

I then had my PowerPoint technician throw a presentation up on the wall. It showed all of the dozen primary areas of concern. I asked who wanted which one. It was silent in the room for a long time. They couldn't believe they were going to get to choose the topics they really wanted.

Why in the hell not? If they were interested enough in something that they would stick their necks out and ask for it, it stood to reason they were probably going to do a pretty damn good job of researching it.

As I closely watched the expressions on their faces during the uneasy silence, I noticed that a short redheaded girl seemed to be shape-shifting before my very eyes. Her eyes opened wider and wider, her face became the vision of inspiration, and, sure enough, she was the first one to throw her hand up in the air. She was looking me right in the eye.

"What is your name, young lady?"

"Mary Catherine O'Sullivan," she replied with all the confidence any twenty-two-year-old could ever possibly hope to have.

"And what area do you choose, Mary Catherine O'Sullivan?" I asked, knowing full well that she was going to pick health care. I was looking at her résumé, which had three different degrees in the health care field from NYU.

"Foreign relations," she replied with a voice full of optimism.

"Holy shit," I mumbled under my breath. I looked at my chief of staff, who was sitting to my right. He straightened up, flipped his folder shut, said quietly, "The very best of luck, Mr. President," and walked out of the room. He could always get really pissy over the smallest things.

"Well, you've got it, young lady. Who's next?"

Mike returned shortly, his composure regained. Forty minutes later, all of the assignments had been made and topic information folders passed out, and everyone seemed happy.

As I looked at the list of assignments, I quickly thought of twenty-five more issues I would have liked to see researched, but that would have to come when the initial topics were complete.

The new Dream Team was formally introduced at the next Cabinet meeting, and instructions were given that required full cooperation from all levels of government—including the Cabinet itself. I explained that the new hires were not there to be spies or snitches. They were there to assemble facts and figures, so they could give me the information I needed to make the best possible decisions.

My last words to the cabinet on the matter were, "If you do not talk to them in a timely fashion, you will be talking to *me* in a timely fashion, and you will not enjoy the conversation."

Mike had rapidly warmed up to the concept, and he and I had gone over the list of issues to be researched before the assignments had been made. We both agreed that there were many more things that needed to be looked at, but the initial list seemed like the right place to start.

The first issue on the list of priority items was national security, which included all four branches of the military and our seventeen different intelligence agencies. Really, seventeen? This assignment also concerned the security of our borders, or, more to the point, the astounding lack thereof, and the history and present conditions of the many terrorist organizations operating around the globe. This topic had gone to a recently returned combat veteran with two master's degrees from the University of Alabama.

The second issue was—thank you very much, James Carville—the economy, stupid. Subcategories included federal government spending, the national debt, jobs, the financial community, and, last but never least, taxes.

My last briefing on the subject indicated that ***the national debt was almost $19 trillion, which represented $58,000 for every man, woman, and child in the United States. There was a quickly approaching point of no return, after which it would be impossible*** *for us ever to pay the debt off. That should be a really fun day on the stock market. Just the interest on the national debt was over $260 billion a year. That would buy a lot of cancer research.*

Forty-seven percent of our national debt was held by foreign countries, with China at the top of the list at $1.6 trillion, Japan at $1.2 trillion, and Belgium at $310 billion. Only 18 percent of our debt was held by domestic private entities, American citizens and corporations.

The thing that really caught my eye was on the revenue side. Revenue for government comes in the form of taxes that you and I, average Americans, pay. *My research indicated that tax breaks equaled $1.24 trillion a year. Tax breaks were little gifts that had been handed out by Congress over the years to the people they were beholden to, and I don't mean the American people. I mean Congress's actual owners and operators, the big greedy special-interest groups. Tax breaks actually represented money being given to those groups, via their not having to pay those taxes. It was actually Robin Hood in reverse: rob the poor to pay the rich.*

I also wondered how many American taxpayers were familiar with that little fact, and what they were going to do about it when I brought it up during my next television address.

This all made me want to go to the Oval Office, crawl under the desk, assume the fetal position, and stay there for the next four years. I would have done this, except that Mike would have taken over my chair and spent all day kicking me.

A bright young man from the LSU School of Business and Finance grabbed this topic with gusto.

The next item on the list had been asked for by a six-foot-six former all-American tackle, who had both a law degree and a PhD in political science. Not to mention a genius IQ. I explained to him that I wanted his dress code to be full pads, a helmet, and the breathing strip across his nose. His area of research would be Congress—and how in the world it had ever gotten into the shape it was in.

In addition to that, he was tasked with evaluating the powers of the president and how they had eroded over the last fifty years. He seemed ecstatic about the opportunity to go head-to-head with the beast itself, and I thought he was probably exactly the right person for the job.

Health care was the next problem we needed to attend to, sooner rather than later. My predecessor had goodheartedly provided some sort of health care for just about everyone, which was a wonderful thing. However, over the course of its inception, universal health care had become watered down, totally confused, and completely unaffordable. Luckily, I had the inside track on this one. My niece was one of the leaders in the field of health care administration, and she understood the complexities of the issue as well as anyone in the country. Also, I had spent a good part of my forty-year career dealing with the ins and outs of the principles of insurance. Once we could figure out the intricacies of doctors, hospitals, medical research, and prescription medicines, there were going to be some changes to the system. These changes would be extremely beneficial to the nation's poor and middle class.

A young University of Missouri graduate enthusiastically volunteered for this assignment, and she looked like she could figure it out with no sweat.

One of the hottest topics of the election had been immigration, both legal and illegal. We needed to find out the true and current status of border security and immigration policies, and we needed to stick our toes into the frigid waters of overpopulation. This was going to be the most emotional and controversial social issue of the administration. Mike had picked the research person he wanted for the topic during his interviews, and when she raised her hand and volunteered for this one, he had a look on his face like he had just won the Powerball. His enthusiasm might have had something to do with her recent graduation from Notre Dame.

Having been accused of being a tree-hugger during the campaign, I knew that the person assigned to researching environmental issues was going to have to sort through very few facts and a lot of greedy people to get to the truth of the current state of the environment. I personally wanted to know why we were losing money when we sold timber off federal lands, and why we couldn't just sterilize some of the wild mustangs in the West and then leave them alone, instead of selling them to people who eventually let them end up in slaughterhouses. The young man from the University of Colorado who chose this topic was also going to tackle clean air, clean water, and, of course, climate change.

A civil engineer from MIT came to our rescue when he volunteered to research our infrastructure. This was another topic that we desperately needed to know the real story on, complete with facts and figures, because this was going to become critical during the next few years of our administration.

American foreign relations had always appeared to me to be something like a Chinese fire drill, no pun intended. Political correctness also not intended. It had always seemed to me that our foreign relations policy had been to try to buy friends, which we all learned from our mothers at an early age is impossible. We also had a history of providing military hardware to people we didn't really like, so they could fight other people we disliked even more, and then those arms recipients would turn their weapons against us at a later date.

I had the feeling that Mary Catherine O'Sullivan could get a handle on the complexities of the topic in very short order.

For a long time, I had assumed that our judicial system was a fairly squared-away system for dispensing justice. But for the last twenty years, that assumption had seemed to wither away each night. I would watch the evening news and be constantly baffled by some local judge who had taken three years to arrive at a totally absurd verdict, or by the Supreme Court—commonly known as the old folks' home for lawyers—getting it completely wrong time after time. I would have liked to have a business-person take on this research instead of a lawyer, but when the Harvard Law kid raised his hand and volunteered, Mike shot me a look that indicated that World War III would start right there if I said anything. He was probably right. It takes a lawyer to catch a lawyer, so to speak.

There's an old country song called "Down on the Border," and I started humming the melody when we picked the person who would research the issue of illegal drugs. The border came into play for national security, immigration, and again for illegal drugs.

The tall young lady from the University of Arizona who volunteered for this topic was happy to be selected, until I threw in a little extra in the form of, "Also, please see what you can find out about why legal prescription drugs are so terribly expensive. I know of a prescription that costs $112 in United States, but you only pay $30 in Canada and $20 in Mexico for the exact same thing."

She hadn't seen that coming, but she was obviously both capable and confident. Her smile told me that although she wasn't offended, I did owe her a favor when the next round of assignments came up.

I don't often get into abstract philosophies, but the concept of Manifest Destiny bothered me. It had always meant to me, *I am bigger than you are, so I get all your stuff.* That and the condition that Native Americans were in today made me wonder how we could have the greatest nation on earth after starting it by taking away other people's lands and thinking of them as inferior human beings, and then treating them like shit for two hundred-plus years. So I wanted to gain some knowledge on this whole subject and indulge myself by having somebody a lot smarter than I was figure it out. I don't believe in racial profiling, but it seemed like a real good fit when the young lady who volunteered for this assignment turned out to be an attractive, intelligent, 100 percent Northern Cheyenne OU graduate. This one was going to be interesting. Also, I knew what her next assignment was going to be. She and the young lady doing research on immigration would be perfect to take on the most important issue in the second round of assignments: race relations in our country.

Last but not least on my list of things that we should all know a lot about was our political system. Not the theory, but the actuality of how we elected our leaders. Did we want people to lead us based on a popularity contest, or based on their abilities? **Politicians were getting sold to the American public, much like automobiles or toothpaste. Lots of smoke and mirrors, glitz, and sound bites—that was what made up our elections.**

Was there a better way? Should terms be longer or shorter? What should the financial limits be? Voters needed to take a long, hard look at how they elected their leaders, and I took it upon myself to be the one to provide them with some honest information for their deliberations.

The world had gone from travel by horseback to travel by spaceship. Communications had changed from the Pony Express to texting. But our political system still seemed to be based on horseshit.

Young Mr. Smith from NYU was ecstatic to get that one.

They were all given their instructional folders, White House passes, and my personal phone number, in case they ran into any stubborn bureaucrats or officeholders.

This was off to a very promising start, except that we did not have a name for them. We solved that later in the day when I started calling them the Dream Team. Mike referred to them as the Dirty Dozen.

OFFICE OF THE PRESIDENT OF THE UNITED STATES

———

LIST OF THINGS TO DO

1. *Develop state-of-the-art information systems.*

2. *Provide method for all Americans to access all government information.*

3. *Establish protocols for identifying important research projects.*

4. *Initiate system for all citizens to provide input for government officials.*

CHAPTER SIX

THE ASSASSINATION

———◆———

The best government is a benevolent tyranny
tempered by an occasional assassination."

— VOLTAIRE

NO ONE HAD MENTIONED THAT only about 150 years ago on
this day, April 14, John Wilkes Booth shot and killed President
Abraham Lincoln. Probably best that I wasn't aware of that historical fact, as I might have just stayed in bed all day and missed
all the excitement.

It took a little while to understand and get comfortable with
the routine of living in the White House. I usually got up around
7 a.m., showered, got dressed, and hit the door of the residence
ready to solve all the country's problems by 8. After the first
couple of months, I had developed an early-morning raid on the
kitchen, which had become necessary because every living being
in the White House had turned into the calorie and cholesterol

police. They had somehow learned that I have a slight problem with elevated blood sugar levels, and they had each individually placed themselves in charge of keeping me away from anything that might taste halfway good.

So every morning, I would walk through the reception office, greet everyone, go into the Oval Office, and then sneak out the side door and down the hall to the stairs that led to the kitchen. Having established a true example of diplomatic understanding with James, the head chef, I would always find a small white box containing two delicious blueberry muffins, which would be waiting on the table just inside the kitchen door. I would pick them up, place them under my arm like an NFL running back, and charge back to my office, where I would immediately eat one with a cup of coffee and hide the other in a desk drawer for later in the day. If I do say so myself, I am good at the fine art of survival.

On the morning of April 14, as I opened the side door into the hall with visions of blueberry muffins in my head, I almost ran into what appeared to be a Secret Service agent. But in a split second, I realized that he just didn't look the part. Secret Service agents are sharp dressers. They're instantly recognizable after you've lived with them even for a short period of time. They also don't have an automatic pistol with a silencer in their hand.

When the door swung open, he was just two feet from me on the other side. We were face to face. A look of surprise crossed his face, followed by one of satisfaction. He started bringing the gun up. His eyes were hard and cruel. I had seen eyes like that a long time ago.

Growing up on the poor side of town meant you got to associate with people with hard eyes on a daily basis. They were called bullies. I had always had a special place in my psyche for them, ever since the first time I'd been beaten up by one. As time went by, I grew into a six-foot-two guy who weighed in at 250 pounds. The bullies no longer wanted anything to do with me. But I still got the distinct feeling that I should be punching out somebody's lights when I saw those cruel eyes.

My first instinct was to slam the door in his face, but there wasn't room or time to do so. His gun was coming up quickly, and my options were evaporating at the same speed. I figured I could just stand there and get shot or_____, so I just sucker-punched the son of a bitch right in the nose as hard as I could. The gun came up to level with me, and then it kept going up toward the ceiling. I guess the pain of his broken nose made him forget to pull the trigger. He fell backward, hitting his head on the marble floor. He lay there for a split second.

As I stood there, stunned, thinking about what a close call that had been and wondering where in the hell the Secret Service was, he raised the gun toward me again. I had no place to go, so I jumped right on top of him, grabbed the gun, and twisted it away from me. We both had fingers on the trigger, so it was impossible to tell who fired the three rapid shots into his chest.

His hand went limp and fell away. I had total control of the gun and pulled it out of his hand.

After laying there on top of him for a couple of seconds I staggered to my feet, covered in blood. I'm not a doctor, so I didn't know if he was dead or not, but I knew he wasn't going anywhere with a broken nose, a concussion, and three slugs in his chest.

I thought for a second about the timing of the whole incident. If he had been a couple of feet farther away, I would not have been able to punch him, and I would be dead.

Standing in the empty, silent hallway, I wondered where everyone was in the busiest house in the country. The door had automatically locked behind me, so I walked down the hall to the reception entrance of the president's office, covered in blood and with a hot pistol in my hand.

When I walked into the office, the first two people to notice me were Secret Service agents, and the looks on their faces were almost comical. They and the other people in the office started moving and making a lot of noise as I tossed the pistol to one of the agents and said, "There is some trash out in the hall that needs to be picked up." I went up to the residence to change out of the bloody suit and take a hot shower.

When I came out of the shower, I was an entirely new man, and one mad SOB. I wasn't in the mood for a suit, so I put on a comfortable pair of Levi's and a sweatshirt. I searched through the unpacked boxes of my personal belongings and found my

Smith & Wesson Airweight hammerless .38 special, with a one inch barrel. I found the shells, inserted five hollow points into the cylinders, and slipped it into my Levi's pocket. There were going to be a few changes around here, of a more personal nature than the ones I'd planned on making for the good of the nation.

When I walked out of the residence, there were nine Secret Service agents standing there instead of the normal two, including the head of the presidential detail.

It had been many years since there had been a serious assassination attempt, although for the past two years, there had been quite a few instances of people jumping over the fence that surrounded the White House and running around the grounds. Once, a man had actually gotten through the front door of the White House. He spent several minutes inside before getting caught.

No one said anything on the walk to the Oval Office, but once we were inside, I turned to the agent in charge of the presidential detail and said, "Thirty minutes from right now, I want to know how that man got in here, and in two hours I want to know who he was."

I then turned to Mike and said, "Effective immediately, the Secret Service is only responsible for the inside of the White House. The outside and the grounds are going to be secured from now on by a US Navy SEAL team. Make it happen, now! And get the head of the Secret Service on the phone."

Two minutes later, the head of the Secret Service was on the phone and apologizing. I told him to shut the fuck up and listen.

"I want two new teams of Secret Service agents providing security for my kids. I want the current ones reassigned, and I want twice as many agents on each team. I want the very best people you have on those details, and I want it done inside of twenty-four hours. If you can't get that done, your successor will." He started talking, but I hung up. He was supposed to be doing, not talking.

It was very quiet in the office at that point. No one, not even Mike, had ever seen me mad before. As a matter fact, I hadn't lost my temper in twenty years. But there are just no excuses for some things, and where I come from, you don't mess with a man's blueberry muffins. That would be the end of the calorie and cholesterol police, and my blueberry muffins would be waiting on my desk for me every morning starting the next day. Oh yeah, White House security would be greatly improved from now on. Hopefully my fears over the safety of my children would be lessened.

Thirty minutes later, I learned that the man had gotten into the White House by hiding in a delivery van. An hour later, I found out that he'd been traced to a terrorist watch list.

I got to be good friends with the SEAL team members and, yep, the .38 special stayed in my pocket for the rest of my time in office, alongside the famous pocketknife.

OFFICE OF THE PRESIDENT OF THE UNITED STATES

———

LIST OF THINGS TO DO

1. *Integrate the Secret Service, Capitol Police, and all other protective forces into one cohesive unit.*

2. *Inspect and modernize White House security systems.*

3. *Start surprise weekly tests of security personnel and equipment.*

CHAPTER SEVEN

HEALTH CARE

———

"It is health that is real wealth and
not pieces of gold and silver."

— MAHATMA GANDHI

I THINK THE MAIN REASON the voters elected a guy with no
experience in politics was that they felt the need for some basic changes in the philosophies and viewpoints of leadership.
Honesty would probably be nice, for a start.

*First of all, we needed to get away from the busi-
ness-as-usual, take-care-of-the-special-interests kind
of thinking, so we could discover new ideas and imple-
ment policies that would improve everyone's life in the
future, instead of making things better for a few extremely wealthy people at the expense of the rest of us.*

*Health care was a perfect example of this precept.
The people with the most money got the very best
health care available, and the rest of us rolled the*

dice and hoped the care we needed was covered by our insurance policies. If this sounds like the right way to do things to you, go explain this philosophy to the parents of a dying child. Please let me listen to your explanation of why people have to be in great pain, with no expectation of any decent quality of life, just because they don't have enough money in their checking accounts to maintain the insurance companies' bloated profit margins.

I wondered how anyone could sleep at night, knowing that human beings were suffering and dying because of their lust for profit.

Several years ago, I stopped to help a young college boy who had been hit by a car while riding his bicycle to class. He was lying in the street, clearly in a lot of pain, but he was begging me not to call 911 because he didn't have any money to pay the hospital and doctor bills. I called for an ambulance and then tried to explain that the guy who hit him probably had insurance, and if not, the medical folks were required to provide help free of charge in cases like this.

I wasn't really sure if that was the case, but it struck me that one's primary concern should not have to be finances when you're lying on hard concrete in a lot of blood and pain.

My basic philosophy of life was that no living thing should ever have to suffer if there was any way to prevent that suffering, regardless of their ability to pay. It was completely wrong to deny freedom from

pain and suffering because of the financial interests of persons or corporations.

The Dream Team report on health care was finished in an amazingly short amount of time. After reading it twice, and after having several lengthy telephone conversations with my niece and several more meetings with notables in the field, I was ready to roll out a new concept in health care.

The entire concept of providing quality health care to every American citizen had always been seen as complex, convoluted, and unbelievably complicated. In reality, it was just a very simple mathematical formula, which had been abused by the greed of, once again, our wonderful special-interest folks. They cared more about lining their own pockets with obscene amounts of money than offering maximum-quality, compassionate care to their fellow human beings.

Our research provided some very interesting facts that needed to be considered.

Present-day health care costs in the United States were $8,612 per capita, the highest in the world. So our quality of care should have been the best anywhere, right? Nope. The Organisation for Economic Co-operation and Development ranked the United States third from the bottom in the thirty most developed countries in health care quality followed only by Mexico and Turkey.

The $389.3 billion health care tab had increased a whopping 64 percent since 1980, which put it at 17.9 percent of GDP—the highest in the world.

Armed with these and many more facts and figures, we set about trying to find ways to fix this mind-numbing problem.

Our basic findings were that all you had to do was take the total dollar costs for necessary health care for all American citizens, and divide that amount by the number of American citizens who could actually afford to pay into such a system.

The kicker was that there were several entities— and layers of bureaucracy—that were not needed in the system. Those accounted for a large percentage of health care costs.

The first one that came to mind was insurance. I am not an anti-insurance person, and I am in agreement with the basic concept of insurance, which is that large numbers of people put money into a giant kitty, which pays for things that individual people could not pay for themselves. In its purest form, this works wonderfully.

The problem was that insurance companies had tremendous overhead and desired very large profits. Plus, it took a gigantic government bureaucracy to keep tabs on and do business with insurance companies because government was doing a lot of the paying for the health care tab.

I figured most people would be willing to chip in a little extra to help prevent the suffering of the less financially fortunate, but I doubted that any of us would willing to contribute to the bloated profits of health insurance companies.

So, long story short, if we took the insurance companies out of the equation and replaced them with a single nation-wide not-for-profit trust—which would also eliminate more than half of the federal health care bureaucracy—we would reduce the total national health care bill by about 39 percent, which will go a long ways toward providing affordable health care for all of us.

The other part of the problem was that, except for the not-for-profit hospitals, most doctors, hospitals, and pharmaceutical companies were also operating on a "let's make a big fat profit" philosophy. Their costs needed to be reined in—into a common-sense dimension.

Part of our information-gathering process included looking into how our good neighbors to the north handled the problem. We had all heard of the horrors associated with so-called socialized medicine, and about the poor quality of medical care associated with the Canadian system. Our research clearly indicated that they actually did have a good health care system, complete with doctors and hospitals equal to or better than ours and shorter average wait times than in the US.

And the whole program was funded through their tax system. This, in itself, reduced costs because there was no need for a separate revenue entity. Each of us paid our fair share of taxes for things like defense, transportation, and law enforcement; in this system, we would also be paying our fair share for health care. I had talked to quite a few Canadian citizens who were more than happy with their health care system, depending on which providence they lived in.

If we were to take the best of the best as a model and make it even better, we would get a common-sense handle on the situation.

One of my pet peeves in life is when anyone tries to solve a problem with a piecemeal approach to the symptoms, instead of a well-planned, comprehensive attack on the entire problem. Many health issues would never arise if we were to practice proper preventive medicine—which would save another 12 percent of the health care bill, not to mention the pain and suffering that should never have occurred in the first place.

The key to preventing medical problems was excellence in research. The way we went about doing medical research was based on close observation of the Three Stooges movies. The Stooges were truly great comedians, and we all loved their unique problem-solving philosophies, but medical research needed a better approach.

Several years ago, we were all shocked to learn that a study had just proven that cranberries caused cancer. This was great news because we really needed to know what caused cancer, and I didn't particularly like cranberries anyway. The problem was that this wonderful information was made public shortly before Thanksgiving, and it was shown to be completely false right after the holidays.

It may not have done much for preventative medicine, but you had to admit that it did a hell of a job on the nation's cranberry farmers.

Medical research was extremely expensive. That was the nature of the beast. So the costs of these studies were almost always born by the companies that would profit from certain outcomes. This in no way provided us with the information we needed on subjects that did *not* provide giant advertising opportunities for whoever paid for the research.

Research needed to be organized and conducted in a manner that would allow us to delve into the key medical issues—which would provide the most improvement in our health care system, not whiter teeth and increased market shares for the makers of the products. It also needed to be done with a goal of honest information, not advertising slogans. Careful gathering of existing statistical data from the VA and other government funded hospitals, along with ongoing future gathering of such information from those institutions, would provide unbiased, lower-cost, accurate information into perpetuity.

I did not believe in being too proud of my own opinion, so for any issue, I always tried to get as much input from as many sources as possible. In this case, I presented my health care ideas to a large group, including my senior staff, the Cabinet, several members of Congress I had come to trust, and members of the health care community.

They all listened without saying a word, and at the end of my presentation, it was so quiet you could hear the proverbial pin drop. When I looked around the room and asked for input, it got even quieter, until one brave soul said in a very low voice,

"You're exactly right, Mr. President, but none of that is ever going to happen. The lobbies from the American Medical Association and the multitude of associations that protect all the entities in the health care system are going to ride you out of town on a rail."

I replied, "It's the first duty of this administration to fight greed and stupidity at every level on every issue. Our whole mission is to fight uncaring and uncompassionate people at home with the same vigor we use to fight terrorists overseas. It's my intention to take the truth of these matters to the American people so that their voices may be heard."

That impassioned little speech didn't change their minds about our chances for success, but it did let them know that the fight was on, and common-sense health care was going to be an important battle in the war against the things that were wrong with our country.

I thought the meeting had gone very well, and I was in a good mood when I went back to the office. Mike had gotten back a few minutes before I had and was looking at a newspaper.

"Well shit," was his comment as I walked up behind him.

'What's the matter now, Michael?"

He showed me a picture in the paper of our secretary of the interior. He was shaking hands with the head of an environmental group—and accepting some sort of token of their appreciation.

The day after the inauguration, I'd made a big point of informing everyone working in the executive branch that no one would accept any gifts or gratuities of any kind, from anyone for any reason. I called the secretary of the interior.

An hour later, he walked into my office, and I asked him right away if he had accepted the gift. He had been an excellent choice for the position, with impeccable credentials and the burning desire to manage our nation's resources in a manner that would be in the best interest of our citizens. I liked him and had a great amount of respect for him, but I had no choice.

I fired him right then and there.

I told him there was no question in my mind that a thirty-dollar knickknack did not constitute a bribe, but the appearance of impropriety was the same thing as impropriety, and rules were rules in this administration. He was gone immediately.

The media jumped on the situation with both feet and turned it into a full-scale news headline. The pundits described it as a knee-jerk reaction from a grumpy old president, Congress demanded an immediate investigation into the whole affair, and the American people started thinking they actually might have found an honest person in Washington.

I had no idea whom to replace the man with, because it had been hard to find someone with his qualifications in the first place. But once again, good old Mike came through in a pinch. Only days before, he had met the woman who was second in command at the Department of the Interior, and he had been very impressed with her intelligence and common sense. She accepted our offer of the position, and within forty-eight hours, it was as if the whole mess had never happened.

I felt bad for the man who had ruined his career for a thirty-dollar trinket, but the integrity of the administration had to be upheld at any cost if we were to earn the confidence of the American people.

OFFICE OF THE PRESIDENT OF THE UNITED STATES

LIST OF THINGS TO DO

1. *Appoint health care task force.*

2. *Devise "best possible" health care model.*

3. *Investigate all financial aspects of medical field.*

4. *Increase medical educational facilities by 33 percent.*

5. *Give preference to American citizens in health care education.*

6. *Develop research studies for all major illnesses.*

7. *Identify funding for all research activities.*

CHAPTER EIGHT

TERRORISM

———•———

"War is a continuation of politics by other means."

— ANONYMOUS

FOR MOST OF MY LIFE, I had been in bed at 11 p.m. and sound asleep by 11:30. The routines of the White House had been keeping me up later, reading briefs and having the occasional late-night meeting. Tonight had been different. I'd finished dinner by 6, I'd polished off reading the daily staff briefings by 8, and I was in bed and sound asleep by 9:30.

A beautiful dream had just been starting to unfold. There were the beginnings of beautiful beaches, cloudless skies, and warm breezes, and I think in the distance there was a beautiful lady walking toward me.

The noises were sudden and loud, and my dream faded with the ringing of the phone, a knocking on the door, and an obnoxious beeping sound I'd never heard before. My eyes finally focused on the clock. It read 2:47 a.m.

"This better be good," I muttered as I look for my pants and shirt. I had not owned a pair of pajamas for several decades, so finding at least a pair of pants before opening the door was imperative. The knocking grew louder, and I jerked the door open to see a very concerned look on the face of the senior Secret Service agent on tonight's detail.

In a strained voice, he said, "They need you in the Situation Room immediately, Mr. President."

"What's up, Frank?" I asked as I searched for my shoes.

"I believe they have just learned of attacks on two of our embassies, Mr. President."

As we started out the door, he held up a light sports coat with the presidential seal on the breast pocket.

"Is it cold down there?" I asked.

"No, Mr. President, but this coat has special tracking devices in it, and we have just gone into a code four condition."

Hell of a way to start a new day.

The atmosphere in the Situation Room was tense as it filled with representatives from the intelligence agencies. The duty officer hurried up to me and started giving me the information I had never wanted to hear.

"In simultaneous coordinated attacks, two of our embassies in the Middle East have been completely destroyed," he said in a low, tense voice.

"Casualties?"

"We have no indication of any survivors." He handed me a book of possible scenarios, which I had asked the Joint Chiefs of Staff to put together several months earlier.

"Do we know who is responsible?"

"Not yet, sir, but we are working on it."

Sitting in my chair at the head of the room, I watched as more and more people hurried through the door and took their assigned positions. I felt the tensions rising with each new arrival.

Forty-five minutes later, the Joint Chiefs had arrived in full uniform, along with the heads of all the intelligence agencies, my chief of staff, and the secretary of defense. Two large coffee urns had also arrived.

I knew things had been going too smoothly.

The tremendous amount of activity going on in front of me boiled down to only one question in my mind: *Who did it?* The *what to do about it?* question had been answered months before, during my planning meetings with the Chiefs on strategic responses to terrorist attacks. We had developed battle plans for many potential scenarios, including what had just happened.

I had taken the matters of terrorism and national security seriously from the get-go. Our responses would be nonnegotiable. There had been many meetings over the past few months during which we had discussed the size and scope of our retaliation, should we be attacked. We had recently been discussing the value of preemptive strikes as opposed to retaliatory attacks. As of tonight, that was a moot point. The only questions were how big the retaliation would be and where they would take place. The response was going to be neither proportional nor long in coming. It would be what I referred to as the "Chicago Way." This entailed: you bring a knife to a fight, I bring a gun.

I was pretty damn sure this had gone on long enough. Now was the time to drop the whole load on them. While everyone else in the room was working at a fever pitch, I was just waiting for positive identification of the idiots who had done it. And I was ready to give the order.

After three hours of watching the activity, and drinking four cups of coffee, I excused myself, citing the need for a restroom break. I instead sneaked outside for one of my clandestine cigarette breaks. I had stopped smoking four years ago, and everyone had been very proud of me for quitting. But like many other people, I occasionally regressed during stressful situations, and this definitely qualified as one.

Since he had given me the tracker jacket, Frank had never been more than an arm's length away from me. He followed me outside.

It was a pleasant night in Washington. Like the song says, there was a warm wind pushing the clouds around. Under different conditions, it would have been nice to be outside listening to the rhythms of the city.

Frank suddenly stiffened and turned away from me. I could hear him having a short conversation with his wrist. He turned back to me and, after hesitating for a second, looked me straight in the eye and said, "They know who did it."

———

Back in the Situation Room, it was deathly silent. Everyone froze as I walked back into the room. They watched me with gazelle intensity.

"Who did it?" I asked.

The response from the NSA director was low, instantaneous, and confident.

"How sure are we?"

"Absolutely, Mr. President," the director replied. "We have undeniable proof, and they've just taken credit for it."

"Are they holding any of our people?"

"There were no survivors, and they are not holding any of our people."

I stood in the middle of the room and watched as they prepared to recite the politically correct responses to this horrific deed. I waited for the white-hot heat of my anger to reach its peak. I thought about all the dead Americans in the burned-out embassies and all the brutalities we had endured from these people over the last decade.

Strangely, my anger subsided instead of increasing, and a feeling of calmness settled over me.

"Here are my orders! Tonight, we owe several debts. The first is to every service person since the Revolutionary War who has died, been injured, or been sent into harm's way in defense of our country, and to their families, who have also served and suffered. We owe a debt to the citizens of our country, who expect us to provide for their safety and security.

"We also owe something to the brutal, savage sons of bitches who perpetrated this barbaric act upon our people and our nation. We will pay our debts immediately, in full."

Walking over to the Joint Chiefs of Staff, I continued, "You are hereby ordered by the commander-in-chief to commence Operation Respect immediately. This entails every facet of Battle Plan Number Six in your book of responses to potential scenarios.

"For the benefit of those of you who have not had an opportunity to read this plan, it entails the use of seven nuclear weapons, to be delivered by both Navy ballistic missile cruisers and Air Force stealth bombers to seven predetermined targets. It also calls for nine days of round-the-clock air strikes on six hundred previously determined targets, consisting of not only military strongholds, but also supply lines, staging areas, communication installations, training facilities, and any financial institutions that have in any way aided the terrorists."

I took a step back, once again looked at the Chiefs, and quietly said, "You have your orders."

I left the Situation Room and walked the halls of the quiet White House, to get rid of some of the adrenalin and regain as much of my normal, demeanor as possible.

It is a hell of a thing to order the use of weapons of mass destruction, and I tried to remember the casualty estimates of the operation. That was the thing I had dreaded the most and prayed would never have to happen. But when my thoughts went back to the senseless and brutal killing of our embassy staff, I could see no other way to handle the situation. I was comfortable with history judging my actions.

After nine long and expensive days, the skill and determination of our Armed Forces was apparent. Every target had been completely annihilated, and following the fourth day of bombing, six of our allies had joined in the air strikes.

Thousands of terrorists had been killed, including dozens of the top leaders. Many thousands more had been wounded. Their training camps, staging areas, and logistical support were gone.

B-52 bombers had dropped millions of pamphlets over enormous chunks of geography, explaining the reasons we had been forced into action. The pamphlets also advised the locals to take up arms against terrorists in their area, to prevent the hell falling out of the sky from happening to them. This proved surprisingly successful, and local citizens in several countries dispatched several thousand terrorists.

Peace groups in the United States protested the use of nuclear weapons, and Congress protested everything because they had not been asked permission to defend our country. Neither group could argue with the success of the operation. People worldwide breathed a big sigh of relief when word of how devastated the terrorists were spread around the globe.

Part of the plan had been to round up all known sleeper cells embedded in the US, which resulted in the immediate arrest for trial or deportation of 1,476 individuals hell-bent on killing Americans at home. Forty-one of those fanatics chose to resist arrest and were killed during the raids.

Opinions from around the globe varied, some supportive, some opposed, but overall the US had gained a new level of respect not seen for fifty years.

Four servicemen and one female chopper pilot had been killed in accidents related to the operation. I attended all of the funerals.

In the six months following the nine days of air strikes, terrorism withered. Very little was heard from terrorists anymore. One political cartoon showed a terrorist beheading someone, and the next frame showed a totally flattened city under a mushroom cloud. The caption read, "The Chicago Way."

Mike once again proved himself to be the smartest guy in the room when he coined the phrase, "Bomb a bank, starve a terrorist."

The terrorists' funding dried up, and groups of sensible people took control in most Middle Eastern countries. And no, I wouldn't allow any taxpayer dollars to be sent over there to rebuild anything. We did encourage the International Monetary Fund to loan enough money to get some of the countries going again.

OFFICE OF THE PRESIDENT OF THE UNITED STATES

———

LIST OF THINGS TO DO

1. Change secretary of state's philosophy and duties.

2. Modernize intelligence and military operations.

3. Increase size of Peace Corps by 100 percent.

4. Continue to expand domestic antiterrorism measures.

5. Increase intelligence information given to local law enforcement.

CHAPTER NINE

IMMIGRATION

———•———

"Give me your tired, your poor, your
huddled masses yearning to breathe free."

— EMMA LAZARUS

IT WAS RAINING HARD WHEN I walked into the office in the
morning. It seemed to rain a lot in Washington in the late winter months. Everyone was muted in their "Good morning, Mr.
President" greetings, except Mike. He was unusually cheery as
he sat with the young lady from Notre Dame who had volunteered to research immigration policies. Mike was explaining his
lifeboat theory of immigration, which I had heard several times
before. He had an awesome IQ and the ability to sell snow to
Eskimos, and he lived to argue a point.

He was explaining that America has always offered a wonderful lifeboat-type opportunity to people from all around the

world who are in difficult situations in their homelands. He then extolled the virtues of the diversity they bring to our country.

"As with all things, there can be too much of a good thing," he was saying as I walked over, getting close enough to hear him put the finishing touches on his impromptu seminar.

"In this case, we are like a lifeboat floating alongside a sinking ship full of good people. We want to take them all onboard and save them from their situation, but if we take on too many, the lifeboat sinks, and everyone is lost, including the people originally in the boat."

He leaned back in his chair and watched her face for a reaction. She thought about it for a couple of moments and then nodded in agreement. Smart girl.

Score another one for the smartest guy in the room. But I was still the president, and he needed to get his butt out of my chair.

In the days following the air strikes against the barbarians who had attacked our embassies, there had been a lot of brainstorming regarding possible retaliatory strikes against us. The amount of damage we had done was tremendous and effective.

The main source of apprehension was the possibility of a CBR attack on American soil. Chemical-biological-radiological warfare was the way the terrorists could hurt us the most. With that in mind, I had ordered a continuation of the original rounding up and detaining of every suspected terrorist in the US. Every federal officer with a gun and a badge was working twenty-four seven, including members of the three letter agencies, the US marshals, and even the park rangers.

I wanted to cut down the potential for mayhem as soon as possible. From the first raids, we had gained a lot of intel on four hundred to five hundred more sleeper cells scattered across the US, but the developing concern was about previously undetected cells coming across the border from Mexico.

I had been closely evaluating the situation of our porous borders and the great potential for disaster they presented since day one, and it seemed to me that there were common-sense reasons to secure our borders. I couldn't imagine why that hadn't happened years ago.

A little research showed that once again, our superheroes in Congress richly deserved a kick in the butt. The congressmen and women had been influenced by their corporate masters, who wanted the cheap labor offered by undocumented workers. They couldn't care less that the average wage for workers in food-processing plants had dropped from nineteen to nine bucks an hour in fifteen years. Congressional pay had increased to well over two hundred dollars an hour during the same time period. And they had no care whatsoever that the taxpayer would have to pick up the tab for health care, law enforcement, and all other expenses tied to illegal aliens crossing our virtually unguarded borders.

These actions by our elected officials would have been called treason twenty years ago.

So Mike started listing the reasons for finally securing our borders:

"Reason one. Thousands of tons of illegal drugs come across our borders every year. These drugs ruin untold thousands of lives and put billions of dollars in the pockets of really nasty criminals in our country. The drug-related costs to both the health care and judicial systems are in the billions of dollars annually. You guessed it, we taxpayers get to pay for that, too.

"Reason two. Illegal immigrants are flooding across the border to the tune of thousands a day. There are an estimated eighteen million people in this country illegally today. They pay virtually nothing into our social systems, but they're soaking up billions of taxpayer dollars. I am not talking about legal immigration; did you catch the word *illegal*?

"Reason three. Since 9/11, we have done a pretty good job of protecting our citizens from terrorists' activities, especially through the screening of people coming into our country through airports. But what good does it do to have secure airports when we have a wide-open border, which thousands of people are paid to carry big bundles across every day? In one day, you could haul everything across the border that you need to destroy a giant chunk of our beloved country.

"Reason four. Several million American citizens who live along and close to the borders are being subjected to terrible, dangerous conditions by the people bringing drugs and people over the border illegally.

"Reason five. Is there any reason we should *not* have secure borders?"

I quietly replied, "No, Mike, I do not believe there is one."

The border between Mexico and the United States runs 1,595 miles from the Pacific Ocean to the Gulf of Mexico. It is guarded by a division of the Department of Homeland Security known as Customs and Border Patrol. The border patrol had started in 1904—when it consisted of seventy-five part-time mounted guards between El Paso and California—and had originally been meant to prevent Chinese people from entering the United States from Mexico. The famed Texas Rangers had been assigned to help them with the passage of the Chinese Exclusion Act in March 1915.

Today's border patrol consisted of 21,394 agents, 10,250 pickup trucks and SUVs, 2,000 sedans, and 205 horses, not to mention helicopters, drones, and a world of high-tech surveillance equipment. **There had been 119 border patrol officers killed in the line of duty since 1904, the most of any federal law enforcement agency.**

Mexican drug cartels offered bounties of up to two million dollars to anyone who would kill a border patrol agent. The border patrol had been the subject of eighteen books, fifteen movies, and six documentaries.

The Department of Homeland Security had another tremendous ace up its sleeve when it came to protecting our borders: the United States Coast Guard.

The Coast Guard had come a long way from the Marine Collector of Customs Duties, started in 1717 by Alexander Hamilton. The 42,000 uniformed men and women and 8,700 civilian employees of the Coast Guard represented the world's twelfth largest naval force and patrol 3.4 million square miles of oceans and waterways. In addition to their rescue operations, which they were famous for, they had eleven primary missions, including migrant interdiction, drug enforcement, and the prevention of terrorists from entering our country.

After several months of briefings on all federal agencies, I was most impressed by the Coast Guard. Their motto, *semper paratus*, meant "always ready," and I was definitely going to take them up on that promise.

The border situation was just the beginning of the immigration discussion.

———◆———

During my third week in office, I had invited the Canadian prime minister to Washington for a weeklong discussion of issues that affected both the United States and our good neighbors to the north.

It was apparent that one of the big issues on his mind was his constituents' strong feelings regarding Canadian immigration policies. A large proportion of Canadian citizens felt that their homeland was quickly being taken over by foreigners from all over the globe. They felt that their way of life was becoming lost forever. Most Canadian citizens were calling for a moratorium on further immigration until a sensible and well-thought-out policy could be put in place.

During these discussions, I had one of the Dream Team researchers do a down-and-dirty poll of Americans. I was validated in my belief that the average American agreed completely with the average Canadian.

The prime minister was in the process of figuring out how to establish a moratorium on immigration, during which the situation could be studied and a more equitable policy established. I felt that the same thing should be done here in the US. I had assigned this project to my legal staff, to research the validity of a moratorium being enacted by executive order.

Might as well give Congress one more thing to snivel about.

America has always been a nation of immigrants from all parts of the world, and the diversity they bring with them is one of the things that make our country great. *However, conditions throughout much of the world had driven millions of people to our country—not because they wanted to be here, and not because they appreciated and wanted to assimilate into our way of life. Rather, they just wanted to escape the chaos back home, and they wanted to change the United States into what they had left, minus the chaos.*

They also, for the most part, expected to be financially cared for, including through education, health

care, and everything else it took to enjoy the American way of life, which we had all worked hard for and contributed to for many generations.

When I brought this up at the next Cabinet meeting, I was not surprised that they all completely agreed to a moratorium on immigration, without exception.

Validation is always great.

One member of the Dream Team made a valid point when she mentioned that she hadn't heard of many people emigrating out of the US.

Many so-called experts in the field had opinions on how to solve the immigration problem. We gathered up all the input possible from all the sources we could find, and we came up with a game plan that actually met the test of common sense.

First, we announced the one-year moratorium on immigration and appointed a nonpartisan blue-chip committee to delve into all aspects, both good and bad, of immigration. We then collected all the information we could about illegal immigration, which turned up some really depressing statistics regarding its effects on crime, jobs, and our overall economy.

This little problem was definitely going to take a tremendous amount of planning and resources to fix.

I invited the president of Mexico to Washington for a week-long meeting, which resulted in signed agreements that would funnel large amounts of capital into Mexico. These dollars would not be gifts from American taxpayers; they would be loans from the International Monetary Fund and investments from business and industry. The funds could only be used for specific projects. At the first hint of any corruption, the money supply would automatically stop, and all funds previously committed would be due and payable immediately.

This system would go a long way toward addressing the abject poverty that has been the main reason why people were enduring the hardships and dangers involved in leaving their homeland. Most of the illegal aliens in our country would rather have lived in their homeland, if only they had a way to make a living there. This was going to be an excellent start to getting them back to a prosperous environment in their own country.

The drug cartels were an entirely different matter. They were well organized, well financed, and unbelievably violent. It took a lot of persuasion to get the Mexican president to let me handle that situation, but he finally agreed in order to get the money.

Thirty-three days after he returned home, the 82nd Airborne Division left Fort Bragg for training exercises along the American border. These training exercises lasted for a month and were backed up by Navy SEALs, Marine snipers, and the United States Air Force. Four months later, the Mexican drug cartels were no longer in existence.

Based on ideas from experts in the field, we also started a giant public works program that would turn the Rio Grande into a series of long lakes. This would be beneficial to agricultural water projects and recreational activities on both sides of the border. The creation of these lakes would produce thousands of jobs for both countries and greatly improve the overall future economy of the Rio Grande Valley.

And the lakes would go a long way toward securing the border—they would be patrolled by the US Coast Guard. In addition to this long water barrier, many miles of fences and other physical barriers would be installed along the border. Most of the central and western two-thirds of the border consisted of remote desert and mountainous regions, which would be patrolled by drones, satellites, and high-tech rapid response teams.

OFFICE OF THE PRESIDENT OF THE UNITED STATES

———

LIST OF THINGS TO DO

1. Completely and immediately secure our borders.

2. Secure all ports and inspect all containers coming into our country.

3. Initiate one-year moratorium on legal immigration.

4. Establish effective penalties for employers hiring illegal immigrants.

5. Assist all individuals who are in the US illegally as they return home.

CHAPTER TEN

OUR ENVIRONMENT

———

"Human history becomes more and more a
race between education and catastrophe."

— H. G. WELLS

SINCE THE FIRST PILGRIMS LANDED on the shores of this country
and cut down trees for firewood, we have been fortunate that
this land has provided clean water, clean air, and all the other
natural resources necessary to build the wonderful civilization
we enjoy today.

However, as our population increased, so did the demand for
these natural resources, and we had come to a point when the
conservation and preservation of our resources was critical for
our survival, not to mention our enjoyment of these finite resources. Without the basics of clean water, clean air, and all our
other wonderful resources, it would not be possible to continue
our way of life.

The Clean Air Act had been in effect since 1955. If you wanted to see how well it was working, all you had to do was fly into LAX and take a look at the smog cover extending over the whole area. The same could be said, to some degree, of practically all our large metropolitan centers.

The reports coming from our western and southwestern states, especially Texas, Arizona, New Mexico, California, and Nevada, painted a clear picture of the quality and quantity of our clean water. They let you know very quickly that not only was there not enough water to meet the needs of citizens and industry—especially agriculture—but the quality of the remaining limited water supplies was diminishing dramatically.

How could this be, in a country that possessed many great aquifers and rivers, as well as adequate annual rainfall in most of the country? Once again, the answer could be found in a combination of the large industries that used and polluted unbelievably large amounts of water; the quickly growing population; and the purposeful inaction of a Congress bought and paid for by the industries that were responsible for the problems in the first place.

Starting to recognize a reoccurring theme, are you?

The solution? It was time for the citizens, voters, and taxpayers of this great country to become aware of the problem—and to let Congress know, in no uncertain terms, that they expected the problem to be remedied for the good of all the people, not just the takers.

The best place to start was for us to demand strict clean air and clean water laws, with strict enforcement and penalties that would actually be a deterrent to those who cared more about their own profits than the well-being of the rest of us. The next step was a sincere effort to switch to electric cars and derive our power needs from solar, wind, and geothermal sources. If these steps were taken, they would represent a tremendous reduction in expenses for the average American, and they would almost completely eliminate our dependency on oil both foreign and domestic. They would also lead to the creation of thousands of new jobs.

I didn't know that I had ever actually hugged a tree (or maybe I'd hugged a cute young elm years ago), but it had always seemed to me that environmentalists were actually people that were smart enough to have a concern for the future of our limited resources, instead of being some sort of boogeymen vilified by the talking butts on the radio twenty-four hours a day.

———————

One of the biggest lies being force-fed the American public by the citizens for a bigger grab was that there was no such thing as climate change. That ship had sailed with all humans with an IQ of twelve or more. We all realized that this was an actual phenomenon—and it would turn into an unequaled worldwide catastrophe if we failed to address the situation.

Why were certain groups denying its existence? Take a look at who's behind the denials and you tell me why.

———————

The main problem with our management of our limited natural resources was that some people were much more interested in getting rich than in providing for future generations. They got in the game early and slapped derogatory labels on anyone who stood in their way. This was a smart ploy on their part, which covered the problem with smoke and prevented any serious discussion of it.

A good example of the resources issue was the Keystone Pipeline. This was a proposed pipeline, owned by Canadian companies, that would run from the Canadian border to the Gulf of Mexico, carrying Canadian oil to ports on the Gulf of Mexico, where it would be put on ships bound for other countries. The smokescreen in this case was that the United States would supposedly reap great benefits in the form of thousands of high-paying jobs. In reality, there would be a few thousand jobs in the construction stage and only fifty full-time maintenance positions after completion.

So the United States would receive very little benefit, but our country would bear the responsibility should anything go wrong—until the end of time. Any spills or disasters would have tremendous economic consequences, and you could damn well believe the American taxpayer would have to pick up the tab, as always. And what benefit would the American taxpayer get for assuming this potential risk? None.

A better question might be: What did the leaders in Congress get for pitching the gigantic fit they did to try to get it passed?

And who was responsible for the tremendous misinformation campaign associated with this operation?

The same was the case for the leasing of federal lands, the sale of timber, and all the other giveaway shows that Congress used to reward their friends, by giving away the things paid for by taxpayers with their hard-earned dollars.

The one thing that upset me the most was when American citizens voted and talked against their own best interests. But that was understandable. It was the result of being lied to and manipulated by special interests for so many years.

Environmental issues were a perfect example. It worked like this.

Greedy people intent on gobbling up all the natural resources they could get their hands on, or polluting the air and water through dirty industrial practices, had the means to prevent the public from seeing what was really happening. So they built a case against the Environmental Protection Agency (EPA), charged with protecting our natural resources. They spread tremendous amounts of misinformation and straight-out lies designed to turn US citizens against their protectors. They'd done such a good job of it that over the years, they had actually made the people they were screwing hate the people trying to protect them.

The Occupational Safety and Health Administration (OSHA) and the EPA exist for one reason: to protect employees and the public from unscrupulous and greedy businesses, which represented only about 10 percent of the business community. Ninety percent of American businesses were honest, patriotic, and well run. They had to pay the price for the jerks, as did the rest of us.

Everyone hated the EPA until Big Ag started building a giant stinking hog confinement operation next door. We then ran crying to them, only to find out that we had signed a petition years ago—given to us under false pretenses by the big guys—that stripped the EPA of its powers to help us.

Had these government agencies made mistakes in the past that led to a giant hole in their credibility? Absolutely! But the bottom line was that they were still there to protect us. They just needed to do a better job of taking care of business.

So we did a common-sense makeover of OSHA and made it 90 percent consultation—designed to help business owners prevent accidents—and 10 percent enforcement activities. This was a 180-degree flip from its previous makeup. It seemed to work well.

In the case of the EPA, it was necessary to leave it as an enforcement agency. We did, however, make their rules both sensible and understandable, and we realigned the monetary penalties to make the penalty fit the crime. The preventive aspects of these changes were instantaneous and beneficial to all parties.

OFFICE OF THE PRESIDENT OF THE UNITED STATES

———

LIST OF THINGS TO DO

1. *Start proactive citizens' environmental advisory board.*

2. *Strengthen clean air and clean water laws.*

3. *Streamline and modernize EPA (based on common sense).*

4. *Start encouraging K–12 students to be conservators of our resources.*

5. *Revise OSHA standards into readable, common-sense rules.*

6. *Make OSHA 90 percent consultation and 10 percent enforcement.*

CHAPTER ELEVEN

FOREIGN POLICY

———

"Now if there is one thing that we do
worse than any other nation, it is to try
and manage somebody else's affairs."

— WILL ROGERS

OUR WONDERFUL COUNTRY HAS ACCOMPLISHED many great
things over the last two hundred-plus years, but our relationships with other countries have not always been among them.

History indicates that in the early days of our country, we
were fortunate enough to establish friendly relations with many
countries, based on mutual respect. But in the last seven or eight
decades, American policy had completely ignored not only the
rules of human nature, but the precept of common sense.

I think we all remember our mothers telling us, when we
were approximately five years old, that you can't buy friends. Yet
we had steadfastly given exorbitant amounts of money to damn

near every country on the planet, and we expected them to let us tell them what to do, just because we gave them money.

And yes, our leaders did love to tell other people what to do. As soon as they got elected to office, they completely forgot the good American voters who had put them there—and the fact that they were supposed to attend to our needs. They were visited on day one by lobbyists for the fat cats, who delicately reminded them who had put up the money to get them elected and what those folks wanted in return for that money. This became especially dangerous when the fat cats were from other countries.

This took up 90 percent of our leaders' time, and they were constantly searching for opportunities to do good deeds—whether they needed to be done or not—to occupy the other 10 percent of their time.

You do remember that they worked only 126 days a year?

So they started doing things that flew in the face of common sense and were diametrically opposed to what their mothers had taught them.

You can't buy friends.
Mind your own business.
Charity begins at home.
If it's not broken, don't fix it.
You don't get respect unless you earn it.

We fought World War II because we had been viciously attacked on the morning of December 7, 1941, at Pearl Harbor.

We decisively won that war in four years' time only because of the indomitable spirit and courage of the everyday Americans who did the fighting and dying for our country. I didn't believe many senators or representatives had fired shots at the enemy during that conflict. Since then, we had fought several wars—over long periods of time—and we hadn't won any of them, because of the lack of resolve of our elected leaders. Our troops fought and died bravely, while our elected officials acted like idiots.

Now we found ourselves in serious trouble at the hands of terrorists. We had either been too nice to them when they didn't have our best interests at heart, or completely ignorant of their true nature. Both conditions had resulted in a lack of respect for the United States, not only by terrorists but by plenty of other countries around the world. Mix in a little greed from some American corporations in dealings with other countries, and you had the ultimate recipe for disaster.

———

With these considerations firmly in mind, during the first week of my administration I had drafted a letter to the leader of every sovereign nation, outlining the philosophy of my administration. I informed them that the United States no longer had any interest in trying to influence the way business was done in their country, or in trying to change their beliefs or philosophies. We would not interfere in their activities in any way.

The letter went on to say that the United States needed to become more economically stable. We needed to pay off our national debt and balance our budget. Therefore, we would no longer be paying them the foreign aid contributions we had in the past. The payments would be discontinued immediately. I even recited the quote, "You can't buy friends." I said we valued their friendship and looked forward to even better relationships in the future, both economically and philosophically.

The last part of the letter said that mutual respect was essential. We had complete respect for them and anticipated their respect for us. And we would not tolerate any disrespect shown to the United States by anyone. Any actions detrimental to the welfare of the citizens of United States would not be tolerated. Overt acts of aggression would be met with instantaneous and decisive retaliation.

After reading Mary Catherine O'Sullivan's excellent report on the current status of our foreign relations policies, and after meeting with many experts in the field, members of the administration realized that a large portion of our foreign relations policies was based on the financial interests of some of America's largest companies. I understood completely that it was in everyone's best interest for our business community to make money, both at home and abroad. But this had been a key factor in getting us into the tremendous jam with other countries we found ourselves in.

So we completely revamped our diplomatic corps and re-placed 47 percent of its employees with new people who had new ideas. They shared a philosophy focused on what was good for the country, not what was good for a few businesses.

The response from other nations was immediate and over-whelming. They were surprised that we could change direction so quickly, and their reaction was completely positive. Even with the elimination of foreign aid—and with the requirements for balance of trade that we had stated in another, earlier letter—most of the other nations had a renewed respect for us. They wanted to be our true friends, not paid-for puppets.

OFFICE OF THE PRESIDENT OF THE UNITED STATES

———

LIST OF THINGS TO DO

1. *Establish a new approach to our relations with all other countries. Treat them as we would like to be treated.*

2. *Create stronger ties with friendly countries.*

3. *Establish much stronger responses to unfriendly countries.*

4. *Immediately stabilize relations with China, Russia, and India.*

CHAPTER TWELVE

THE JUDICIAL SYSTEM

———

"Justice is blind, and quite possibly
deaf and dumb also."

— MARK TWAIN

OUR ATTEMPTS AT REFORMS THAT would make the government
responsible to the American people were proving to be problem-
atic, to say the least. It's hard to make people accountable when
they're the ones who get to make the rules, and when they're
very protective of that right. Over the last fifty years, Congress
and the judiciary had insulated themselves from the will of the
people in every way imaginable.

We thought the legislative branch was hard to reform, but
we had no idea what hard was until we started suggesting some
common-sense changes to the judiciary.

What could possibly be worse?

Mike answered that question in our morning briefing.

"Mr. President," he began in a depressed-sounding voice. "The members of the Supreme Court serve until they die and answer only to their own bloated egos. Who would've thought that someone had a better deal than Congress?"

"You're an attorney, Mike," I responded. "You're supposed to stick up for your own profession."

No response. He just stared at me with a, you-know-better-than-that, look on his face.

During the first week of my administration, I had floated a trial balloon by mentioning in a speech that American citizens should start considering changing the terms of Supreme Court justices, so they would serve only one fixed term of five years. This was met by a 91 percent approval rating from our citizens.

My own primary staff of approximately one hundred people had only nineteen lawyers, a very low number for Washington, DC. But even so, they staged a sizable mutiny in my office the next morning. It lasted all of fifty-nine seconds, at which point I reminded them that they served at the pleasure of the president, and right then, the president was not pleased. If they really wanted to push their point, they needed to do it in writing, and I would review it at a later date. I ended up with three snotty memos and sixteen pouty lawyers. After two weeks, they realized I was right and got over their bad selves.

I delivered the same message several different times and several different ways. The American people caught on to what I was trying to do and jumped on the bandwagon. The ideas were polished further and overwhelmingly approved by a constitutional convention. The Supreme Court justices would now each serve one term of five years. They would take off their little halos and cute little robes and go back to trying to make a living like the rest of the American people.

Next on my judicial agenda was an overhaul of all our court systems, from the smallest municipal court all the way up to the Supreme Court itself. The few changes I asked the American people to consider were simple, but they would go a long way toward solving the problem of crime in the United States. Prevention, rather than punishment, would be the focus.

I asked for a doubling of all mandatory sentences for all crimes involving the use of a firearm, with no variances or plea bargains to let lazy or overworked prosecutors cut deals. And I recommended that the clock start running on the date of arrest; the suspect would be charged, tried, and convicted or set free within a six-month period. This would be accomplished by establishing three new categories of courts, based on the severity and nature of the crime: one for violent crimes, another for nonviolent but serious crimes, and the third for all other crimes.

These changes would be paid for by implementing new rules regarding the incarceration of criminals. Prisons would no longer be comfortable institutions with lots of leisure time. Each and every person convicted of a crime would spend every day of his or her sentence working on projects, which would pay for the costs of incarceration. All penal institutions would be completely self-sustaining. It was estimated that some would even be able to turn a profit. Profits would be given to a fund for the victims of crime.

The largest problem in the judicial system was illegal drugs, so we legalized marijuana for a three-year test period to determine what effect the decriminalization of marijuana would have on the country. We increased monetary and sentencing penalties by 400 percent for all other drug violations.

Anyone convicted of a class A federal felony would not only have the fruits of their crimes seized; all their other worldly assets would be forfeited too. This would slow down the illegal drug business and reduce the number of crimes committed by unscrupulous high rollers and gangsters.

It was going to be a long, drawn-out fight, with Congress once again playing the game of Follow the Dollars.

In the end, the American people did have their say, and our judicial system was improved. But it still needed further reform, which would only be accomplished with fewer lawyers and more common people in Congress.

OFFICE OF THE PRESIDENT OF THE UNITED STATES

———

LIST OF THINGS TO DO

1. Limit Supreme Court terms to one five-year term.

2. Establish independent review board for Supreme Court.

3. Impose three-year moratorium on enforcement of cannabis laws.

4. Start research studies on effects of #3 above.

5. Quadruple fines and prison time for all other drug offenses.

6. Increase seizure laws to include all assets of violators.

7. Establish common-sense recall procedures for all judges and prosecutors at all levels of government.

CHAPTER THIRTEEN

DIVERSITY

———

"The will of the people shall reign supreme."

— ANONYMOUS

THE QUICK START TO EACH day in the White House started with my flipping on the TVs in the bedroom and bathroom and getting the early morning news, while I showered, dressed, and otherwise got ready for the day. The daily news didn't exactly set the tone for the day, but it usually gave me an indication of how things were going to go.

This morning's news was like a constantly recurring nightmare. Another young unarmed black man had been shot and killed by a police officer. The news anchor was delving into the events that surrounded yet another tragedy of this kind.

While displaying my mastery over the double Windsor knot, I kept thinking that the details of the events would do nothing to prevent another lose-lose situation. If the kid was at fault, two lives were wasted. He was dead, and the police officer would never be the same after having killed an unarmed young person. If the kid was innocent and the police officer was at fault, two lives were wasted. The kid was dead, and the police officer was in deep shit.

At the morning press briefing, the assembled news people would be as usual: sad about the death of a young person and happy to have some sensational news to report. They would want to know the feelings of the president and how he was going to stop what had been going on for the last hundred-plus years.

So I did what I always did when presented with a problem. I sought honest information. When I got downstairs to the office, I pulled out the Dream Team report on diversity and read it again, over coffee and my coveted blueberry muffins. I reread the report to see if there was some solution not only to today's tragic events, but to the entire situation surrounding race relations.

The report was actually a combination of three reports put together by a young black man, a middle-aged Native American woman, and an exceptionally intuitive young man of Chinese and Irish descent.

According to the report, diversity in the United States started the second the first explorers set foot on American soil. The first explorers and pilgrims came from Portugal, France, England, and many other countries. At that time, the only culture here was that of the Native Americans, who became known as Indians because the early explorers thought they had arrived in India. No GPS in those days. Since then, people from every corner of the planet have come to this continent with hopes and dreams of a better life, bringing with them different foods, religions, and their own unique cultures. Although most of the 319 million inhabitants of the United States had been born in this country, only 2,932,248 of us—Native Americans—could trace their ancestry in America back more than ten generations, according to 2010 census data.

Since day one of colonization/immigration, we had dealt with the indigenous people in this country with a philosophy of Manifest Destiny, which actually meant, "I'm bigger than you are, so I'm taking all your stuff." We had lied to, cheated, and killed Native Americans with almost no remorse for most of the three hundred-plus years we had inhabited this country. Now these once proud people were confined to tiny pieces of usually worthless land they had never wanted in the first place, and they lived in conditions of abject poverty and hopelessness. A very small percent had beaten the odds and had been assimilated into the new American culture, at the very high cost of losing their culture and heritage.

The report went on to say that it was very obvious that something needed to be done to right this wrong. There were many court cases pending that might bring some small measure of relief to the descendants of the only indigenous people of this country. But given the length of time that had elapsed since the original crimes, and given the current financial condition and mood of the country, not much was likely to happen unless a sitting president took on the issue as a personal crusade.

Hmm, I wonder who would do that.

We initiated a comprehensive program that included low-interest small business loans specifically tailored to Native American businesses. The proprietors received a reasonable preference in all items purchased by governments, and they had our assistance in establishing very lucrative Native American tourism enterprises. People from all over the world flocked to Indian reservations around the United States. They stayed in their hotels, ate Native American foods in their restaurants, and paid the big bucks for guided tours through the natural wonders found on the reservations.

Several new high-tech manufacturing facilities owned by the Cheyenne, Sioux, and Apache nations opened on the reservations. Some of them made parts for NASA's next generation of space exploration vehicles.

"Buy American" took on a whole new meaning.

Modern, highly efficient colleges and trade schools were set up on almost all of the reservations. These would assure continuing success for Native American youth into the future.

The next section of the report addressed the history and current condition of African Americans. It gave a lot of interesting information on how native tribes in Africa captured individuals from other tribes and sold them to white slavers, who in turn shipped them across the ocean in inhuman conditions and sold the survivors to plantation owners in the southern part of our country. Please remember, however, that this was not just the fault of the South. The White House had been built by slaves, and yes, that did bother me a lot.

I didn't need to read the report to know that slavery was very wrong, and the social problems we were experiencing were a direct result of the sins of greedy people from years gone by. Had there been no slavery, and had people from Africa immigrated to our country in a more normal manner, our race relations problems would have been a tiny fraction of what they were, and our philosophies concerning those relations would not have been clouded by guilt, fear, and misunderstanding.

The report went on to discuss the diversity resulting from people of many other countries immigrating to the US over the years. I was amazed to learn that the border patrol had originally comprised seventy-five part-time mounted officers, charged with the duty of not letting Chinese immigrants cross the border between Mexico and the United States. (Now our business community just sent the Chinese most of our money and thousands of jobs, in return for poor-quality and sometimes dangerous products often made by child labor—which is illegal in most developed countries today. And our government is in debt to China a mere $1.6 trillion.) No problem there.

So what was my informed, creative, and wonderful solution to the tragic killing of the unarmed black man? I didn't have the slightest clue. But we need to come up with something morally correct and actually doable that made common sense, and in a hurry.

The way to solve a problem is first to identify the problem. I always try to write down a description of a problem, making it as complete and accurate as possible. Then I try to separate the symptoms from the actual problem and make a list of them, knowing that when the problem is solved, the symptoms will automatically disappear.

I knew this was one issue where separating the problem from the symptoms would be both difficult and critical to finding any successful remedies. Symptoms were plentiful: crime, protests, riots, gangs, dismal living conditions, large percentages of broken families, single mothers with too many children to feed, unemployment, lack of education, lack of hope. All were symptoms, but which ones were the actual problems?

In this case, the problem was the relationship between African Americans and the rest of the citizens in our country. Since the 1960s, many laws had been passed outlawing racial discrimination and providing equal rights for all Americans, regardless of the color of their skin. Overall, it appeared that today things were much better.

But there was a giant problem simmering just below the surface of our society. We saw evidence of this on the nightly news in the form of black on black crime, white cops shooting unarmed black suspects, and reports that about 90 percent of our prison populations were African Americans. Total employment in the United States was approximately 7 percent; unemployment among African Americans was something like 30 percent.

There were some basic and fundamental differences between African Americans and the rest of the population that needed to be identified and understood. This was an extremely sensitive area, and it was going to be very difficult to get a handle on.

Personally, I had three good friends who were African American. We enjoyed each other's company and were completely candid in our discussions, but none of us could figure out the ultimate solution to the problem.

So it was back to the Dream Team. Three exceptional Dream Team members were wrapping up their initial assignments and would be ready to begin research within the next month.

I thought the place to start was with education and employment, the two most important issues to work on to give African Americans a shot at moving up in American society. With better education and more employment opportunities, they would be thought of differently by the rest of American society. And most important, they would have a more positive feeling about their future prospects.

OFFICE OF THE PRESIDENT OF THE UNITED STATES

———

LIST OF THINGS TO DO

1. Eliminate Bureau of Indian Affairs.

2. Initiate Council of Native American Business Opportunities.

3. Establish regional councils to develop minority business.

4. Develop specialized local schools to work with minorities.

5. Start a formal nationwide discussion re: race relations.

CHAPTER FOURTEEN

OUR POLITICAL SYSTEM

———

"Leadership must transcend party politics."

— THOMAS JEFFERSON

MY FIRST ENCOUNTER WITH OUR political system had come when I was thirty years old. I was sitting in a friend's office, drinking a cup of coffee and enjoying the day, when Mike, now my chief of staff, walked into the office and said, "No one has filed for Fourth Ward city councilman. Filing closes in two hours, and we need to get someone on the ticket."

All the other guys in the room were interested in politics except me, and they began trying to think of someone who lived in that ward, whom they could con into running. After an hour without success, someone looked at me and asked, "Didn't you just move?"

I had, in fact, recently moved into the ward in question, and by the end of the day, I was a candidate for a political office.

To make a long story short, I won the election and developed an intense dislike for politics. I had never seen myself as a leader. I was just a regular guy doing a job to help out my fellow townspeople.

At the end of one two-year term, I was narrowly defeated in my halfhearted reelection bid, and nobody was happier than I was.

Since I had been there and done that, even in a minuscule way, I was a much more astute observer of all things political than I had been before. From time to time, the thought would run through my mind that if I were in the office they were talking about on the television news, I would do things differently. Government by the people, of the people, and for the people was always the governing thought in my mind as I watched the obvious greed and frequent insidious stupidity of our elected leaders.

That begged the question, *how did these people get into office?*

The answer was obvious, and it pointed straight to our political system itself.

The first step in our political system occurred when people who wanted to hold elected offices garnered support from the right people in their chosen political parties. They then filed for office and began the all-important fundraising activities, eventually getting endorsements and money from all the right people and becoming packaged and branded so they could be marketed—much like tubes of toothpaste. With each of these activities, they became more and more indebted to their backers and supporters, so that by the time they were elected, their souls and votes were completely controlled by the people who had put them in office.

This was true from city council positions in the smallest towns all the way up to the presidency itself.

The first time around, I had been too naïve to understand the way the game really worked, and I routinely voted against the best interests of the people who had financed my campaign. That made for a very tedious and unpleasant two years and assured my defeat in the next election.

This time, things were completely different. I had made it very plain to everyone from day one that if they supported me in any way—especially if they gave me financial help—the only thing they could expect in return was good, clean, honest government. If they wanted more than that, they needed to back someone else.

My becoming the president of the United States was an aberration caused by Congress, whose members fought not only along party lines, but within parties too, to the point where they couldn't get anything done for the good of the country. Under those conditions, the president was completely powerless. The Senate and the House of Representatives spent all day every day pointing fingers at each other and blaming the president for their inability to function. That, of course, did nothing to help American citizens, who were in need of an honest and efficient government that would provide a strong economy and effective national security, to say the least.

After many years of this becoming worse each year, we the people were desperate for change—real change that would get the country back on course. In 2016, the people of the United States were completely sick and tired of bought-and-paid-for politicians and a bickering Congress. So they decided to dump the professional politicians and have a shot at letting an average, everyday American run the country.

———•———

The roses in the Rose Garden were just starting to bloom as the weather changed from winter to spring. I had always loved the outdoors, and I started having meetings outside, while letting the dogs search for nonexistent bunnies among the flowers.

During one of these early-morning meetings, I asked the senior staff for their opinions regarding the most important things we could do to get our country on the right course again. Each quickly jotted down a list and gave it to Mike. When he gave me the lists later that morning, I noticed he had titled them: "What Else is New?" These were exactly the same things he and I had talked about on a daily basis since arriving in Washington. It was not new information, but it was a validation of our ideas. The items looked like this:

— *Congressional term limits. Members of Congress needed to be limited to serving one five-year term each.* True, there was an argument to be made for experience, but the disadvantages in terms of influence-peddling and disassociation with mainstream America far outweighed the experience argument. We would not permit five years as a representative and then another five as a senator. There would be only one five-year term in any office, and then they would go home and act like regular people.

— *Campaign finance reform. Contributions to the campaign of any person seeking any public office in the United States must be capped at $100.* Campaigns were long on expensive marketing and short on issues. Capping contributions would reverse that trend, and we could all go back to watching TV during the last month of an election without a barrage of commercials. During the previous election, one multibillionaire had publicly bragged that he was going to spend a billion dollars to buy a president. The power of the billionaires' club and the giant political action committees of the special-interest groups had taken the electoral process completely away from the American public. *In order to get the power back to the people, we had to take the big money out of the equation by setting a limit of $100 as the maximum contribution that any person, firm, or corporation could make to a candidate for any federal elected office. Sound too restrictive? Has to be in order to work!*

– *Strict laws prohibiting influence-peddling.* There is an old saying that we have the best government money can buy. I used to think that was funny, until I realized it was true. Regardless of party affiliation, the top layer of Congress was, and had been for many years, completely bought and paid for by special-interest groups. Mike had mentioned several times that 58 percent of congressional office holders were millionaires. The way to stop influence-peddling was to pass laws with strict penalties for buying or selling any considerations from or to elected officeholders. These penalties would include removal from office upon conviction and mandatory prison sentences for both the buyers and sellers of political influence.

– *Recall provisions for all federal elected officeholders.* The Supreme Court had ruled that recall petition laws were unconstitutional. So a constitutional convention—which many people had been demanding—would have to become a reality. It would devise a fair and simple procedure for voters to quickly remove from office any elected official who didn't live up to the voters' expectations. Just like anyone else with a regular job.

– *A balanced budget provision.* In addition to the items previously mentioned, this concept had also been included in the documents of our founding fathers from the original constitutional convention, only to be left out of the final draft for unknown reasons. A balanced budget provision was the only way to get government spending back under control again and eliminate the dangerous national debt. It had to be written with strict language that prevented Congress from deficit spending in any manner.

— *National elections.* The current method of electing a president was much more like a three-ring circus than a function of democracy in action. The state caucuses and primaries only served to increase the costs of elections, to the point where you had to be backed by millionaires to even be a contender. We had to come up with a much better system if we were going to enable average Americans to become our leaders in the future.

OFFICE OF THE PRESIDENT OF THE UNITED STATES

———

LIST OF THINGS TO DO

1. *Establish nonpartisan board of regular citizens to develop a plan for improving our election process.*

2. *Make the case to all Americans for the desperate need for a constitutional convention, which would address term limits, influence peddling, strict campaign finance limits, the recall of federal elected officials, and a balanced budget amendment.*

3. *Develop a modern model for primary and general election cycles.*

CHAPTER FIFTEEN

THE GREAT AMERICAN SPIRIT

———

"Democracy must be a participatory activity by
an informed electorate in order to be successful."

— PRESIDENT HARRY S. TRUMAN

THE BEST THING ABOUT DIGITAL clocks is that you can see them
at night and know exactly how much sleep you're missing. Tonight
was one of those nights, or mornings, to be more exact. It was 4:09
a.m., and I had been staring at the clock since 3:14. When this happened to me back home, I would walk around the house, drink a
glass of milk, and be back in bed and sound asleep in thirty minutes.

But you couldn't do that in the White House. The ghosts
of former presidents teamed up with the challenges of the day
and caused your mind to click on, making sleep impossible.
So I got up, got dressed, and started wandering around the
halls of this truly magnificent old house. It was a warm night

considering the time of year, and I wanted to go outside, but since the day I had assigned outside security duties to a Navy SEAL team, walking around the White House grounds in the dark had become potentially hazardous to your health. I worked my way up to the roof to see if the night-watch snipers were awake and vigilant. They were, and as always, they were great to talk to. Plus, the view of Washington, DC, from the roof of the White House in the predawn hours was nothing short of spectacular.

These guys were completely equipped to host a predawn party. They had hot coffee, fresh donuts, and night-vision spotting scopes that enabled you to clearly see a tiny mouse at two hundred yards, in the dark no less.

I had been forty-seven years old when the officer in charge of tonight's detail was born, but as he shared his coffee with me in the silent predawn hours, there were no differences between us. We were both serving the country we loved and believed in. I asked him what made a person go through the unbelievable rigors required to become a Navy SEAL.

"Mr. President, I think most of us start out looking for the glory and prestige of being a SEAL, but no one finishes SEAL training unless they have a deep, abiding love for this country and an honest desire to defend its people and their beliefs."

Some hot coffee must have gotten caught in my throat, because when he said that I got a little choked up. A picture of the honesty and goodness of the spirit of the American people became crystal-clear in my mind.

Dealing with prejudiced, greedy, and uncaring people could make you become jaded and lose touch with the greatness of the American spirit. The officer made me realize that was what was wrong with professional politicians. Because of who they were and what they did, they lost touch with the everyday Americans who made this country what it is today: the greatest nation on earth. ***It was not the movie stars or the politicians who defined the American spirit. It was the honest, hard-working, free-thinking, fun-loving, everyday American men and women.***

The blood in our veins came from our forefathers, who settled this country with an axe, a plow, and a deep, abiding love of freedom. As they moved westward across this great nation, their tools were a saddle, a six gun, and the courage to be honest and humble while fighting blizzards, wild animals, and overwhelming adversities of every kind.

So the question became: Were we still that kind of people? Did we understand that we owed a great debt to the millions of people who sacrificed so much to get us to where we are today?

I think the answer is that most of us *are* that kind of people. Some Americans have become so focused on their everyday lives and the pursuit of what they perceive to be happiness that they have failed to look around and see where they came from—and the direction they should be going in.

I believe that most of us understand that the true greatness of our country comes from past generations of everyday Americans, who not only fought and died in the wars that made us free, but who invented the automobile, walked on the moon, and accomplished all the things that have gotten us to where we are today. Average Americans. Not the rich, greedy fat cats, and certainly not the politicians.

I also believe that Americans understand that the intangible assets of our country are the most important ones.

Life, liberty, and the pursuit of happiness are more than just words in a famous quote.

———

I thanked the Seals for their service to our country and asked them not to use me for target practice as I walked around the grounds of the White House. I took off down the steps toward the front door.

When I reached the main entryway, I stopped and looked at the picture that hangs there. It depicts Marines raising the American flag on Iwo Jima. If you know the history behind the raising of the flag over one of the hardest-fought battlegrounds of World War II, you will understand the terrific sacrifices our predecessors made to give us our freedom and way of life. The thought of us losing the way of life these brave men and women worked and fought so hard for, of having it stolen from us by the greedy and selfish among us, made me so flipping mad that I wanted to order an airdrop of the 101st Airborne on Wall Street. Maybe I would just send the vice president over there. The outcome would be the same. She had proven her ability to handle those folks.

The sky was changing from pitch black to a predawn gray as I made my way through the Rose Garden, down along the fence that separates the people's house from the realities of the lives of the people who pay the tab for the house—and the government—which is supposed to assure them their inalienable rights.

It was the last day of my first year in office, and while I was very proud of the many things we had already achieved for the good of the people, the upcoming day's events weighed heavily on my mind.

I was to address the nation in a televised speech that would bring the key issues to a head, outlining the items we had to address immediately if we were going to change the course of the country.

I was going to explain to the American people that our country could not survive much longer without a balanced budget, true debt reduction, term limits for Congress, and a closing of the door on people buying the hearts and souls of the members of Congress. These were the most important changes that needed to be

made to our government, and they could only be made by voting, taxpaying US citizens. They were the only ones with the power to bring about these changes.

It was up to me to explain to the American people that I would spearhead the campaign to get these things done, but that in no way did the office of the president have the power to accomplish them. According to our Constitution, only the American people themselves could make these kinds of changes.

Four hours later, when my speechwriters, whom I had nicknamed Hemingway and Michener, arrived for work, I had six pages of facts, hard figures, and pure emotion scribbled out in my yellow tablet. At the end of another three hours, Hemingway and Michener had polished my thoughts into words that would, we hoped, be able to mobilize the good people of our great country, to encourage them to reclaim our country from those who had failed to understand its spirit and had tried to turn it into their own personal monopoly game.

I was going to throw down the gauntlet in the televised speech that would take place that night. I would detail Congress's abuses of American working folks, which would have been deemed nothing short of treason twenty years ago. But in today's world, our elected leaders had subjected us to such a daily barrage of malfeasance and actual corruption that we had become used to it. The establishment's well-oiled machine of blatant lies and disinformation was working perfectly.

I intended to point out the problems that were obvious to everyone, beginning with Congress's inability to balance the budget or even pass a budget bill in a timely fashion. Many times in the past few years, the government had supposedly been forced to shut down because Congress couldn't quit fighting with itself long enough to fund its operations. Even the twenty-four-hours-a-day news networks had a hard time covering all the petty fights, political bickering, and downright stupidity that the men and women of Congress were constantly engaged in. This in itself was totally unacceptable, but when you looked at the rest of the picture—the gifts, the special privileges, the under-the-table payoffs, and the complete disregard for quickly approaching potential disasters, like further terrorism and the national debt's point of no return—you understood that these actions actually constituted treason. At least they did in my mind, and that's what I was going to tell the American people.

I had no intention of just whining and crying about the problems. I was going to lay out the steps that we, the American people, needed to take to correct each of these situations. Those steps started with items that had been in the original drafts of the Constitution, but that were left out from the final version. There were already several organizations trying to initiate a constitutional convention—under Article V of the Constitution—which would deal with congressional term limits, a balanced budget amendment, and provisions to stop any kinds of bribes or rewards to members of Congress from any entities trying to influence legislation, especially foreign countries. A show of support from the president would go a long way toward helping those organizations be successful.

There were a lot more details to be covered, but those were the main points I needed to get across to the nation, to get us headed in the right direction again.

When Mike had finished reading the first draft of the speech, he frowned at me and said, "You're not Irish, but you sure know how to start a fight."

"The voters didn't send us here to hoe the bloody Rose Garden, Michael, me boy," I replied lightheartedly. "The greedy and corrupt folks started this fight many years ago. We're here to finish it."

It had been my practice since day one of the administration that no copies of speeches would be made available to anyone before I delivered them, and there would be no leaks concerning their content. Since the media had no clue what I was going to talk about, they had speculated about every possibility.

Surprise surrounded my impassioned plea for help from the rank-and-file American people, giving extra emphasis to the message.

When the grassroots organizations that had been advocating a constitutional convention learned that the president was going to spearhead the effort, they went into full-speed-ahead mode. They doubled their memberships and funding in three weeks.

Under normal circumstances, I never would have run for any public office, much less the presidency. What made me decide to do so was hearing people say, *"America has seen its best days." The other thing that really upset me was when my friends expressed real fear for the condition America would be in during their children's and grandchildren's lives.* The concerns of the people I talked to were legitimate, and the chances of our current so-called leaders fixing them were minuscule. That's when I knew that we the people had to take back control of our country.

Thousands of people have bravely fought and died since George Washington crossed the Delaware River. Millions have made sacrifices of one kind or another in the hope of creating a more perfect nation—one that would be able to fulfill the dreams of future generations.

The thought that their lives and all of their struggles may be in vain, because of the greed and stupidity of a few citizens today, is more than I can bear.

We must respectfully acknowledge the lives of our forefathers and the sacrifices they made for our country—not just on Memorial Day, but every day—by the way we live our lives. Most of us do not have to walk into harm's way or make great sacrifices in order to carry on the American tradition. We can do our part by voting, speaking to our friends about the importance of these issues, and signing petitions that will change our government.

———————

Immediately after my speech, the American spirit came alive. A constitutional convention was organized and held. The American people understood the need for change. They became mobilized and vocal.

Most people wanted to limit Congress to two six-year terms. I knew that experience could be a virtue, but disassociation with average America and temptations from big-money cats would take place long before twelve years had passed. A bad elected official could do a hell of a lot more harm in twelve years than an honest one could do good in that amount of time. I worked hard for one four-year term. We finally settled on one five-year term and no eligibility to serve in any other elected national office.

A balanced budget amendment and campaign finance reform passed in the convention with no problem.

An amendment prohibiting all gifts and remuneration for elected officials and government employees was a pitched battle from day one. I had to go back to the people and ask for their help twice before we finally agreed on an amendment that would eliminate graft and corruption in Congress for all time.

If two heads are better than one, then 319 million voices are the perfect solution to any ills that democracy might encounter.

OFFICE OF THE PRESIDENT OF THE UNITED STATES

LIST OF THINGS TO DO

1. Develop a much better, more personal way of teaching American history in K–12.

2. Be more proactive and positive in remembering and emphasizing the many things our ancestors have done for the good of the whole world in the past three hundred years.

3. Establish a business plan that will, in the best common-sense ways, guide future leaders to lead our country for the next fifty years.

EPILOGUE

───── ◆ ─────

LAST WEDNESDAY MARKED THE END of exactly three and a half years in office . . . so I quit.

Our country was not in a perfect condition when I left office, but we had accomplished almost all the things that needed to be done in order to give control of the government back to the American people. I had gotten elected so I could accomplish something, and now I was getting the hell out of the way to let the next guy or gal have a chance to accomplish something *else* for the good of the people.

Besides, I wanted to go home. I had spent my entire life on the banks of a big river, under gigantic sycamore and oak trees. I missed the sound and smell of those trees when a gentle summer breeze blew through their leaves.

I knew and liked—and was liked in return by—most of the folks in a fifty-mile radius of my little brick house, on my quiet, tree-lined street. I was not exactly homesick, but Washington, DC, was no match for Hometown, USA.

I had no qualms about abandoning the office. I knew it would be in the hands of the most capable vice president ever to become president.

When we first met, she was a senator. She had been fighting the greedy fat cats on Wall Street on behalf of the average Joe for twenty years. Her ideas and efforts were a big part of the reason why our policies had been insightful and our work successful. She was much better at almost all the things necessary to be a successful president than I was.

I don't think she would have done the things I'd done to eliminate the terrorist problem—or in the way I'd done them—but she had accomplished more than anyone else could have in putting the brakes on the high-finance fat cats, before they drove us over another cliff. And we probably would not have won the fights for term limits, meaningful campaign reform, and a balanced budget amendment without her guidance and heavy lifting.

The American citizens had become used to our message of change, which had originally been a call to arms. It needed a new spokesperson in order to remain effective, and she was the best you would ever find. She was intelligent, outgoing, and extraordinarily popular with the American people, and she had no time whatsoever for the greedy and stupid people who still had no interest in the future of our country or its citizens. She met all the qualifications I originally outlined as necessary to hold the office of president.

Yep, she was damn near as tough as I was, and a hell of a lot better looking.

My leaving office meant she would automatically jump the "first woman president hurdle." The voters would have six months to get used to seeing her in action as president, which would allow her to run as a popular incumbent. So I went home.

The media was so confused that they were interviewing each other, trying to figure what I had to gain by leaving. I explained that you don't have to gain something by your every action. Sometimes you just do something because it's the right thing to do. They never got a handle on that philosophy. They figured I was dying. I really did not mind disappointing them on that item.

Thank you for buying and reading my book.
I appreciate it!
- Fred Seaman

Now get off your ass and go do something to help save your country, before it's too late!

Get involved in your own future. Volunteer, donate, work, talk, at least vote, please!

About the Author

FRED SEAMAN IS A MEMBER of the Writers Guild of America and the Columbia chapter of the Missouri Writers Guild.

He lives in Columbia Missouri with a rescue dog named Stretch and is the father of two truly awesome children, a son Eric, and daughter Gail.

This is his second book and was written because of his uncompromising belief in democracy and a deep abiding love for the United States of America and all that it stands for.